Journal up the Straits

Herman Melville

Herman Melville

Journal up the Straits

October 11, 1856 — *May* 5, 1857

Edited with an Introduction by

RAYMOND WEAVER

NEW YORK
COOPER SQUARE PUBLISHERS, INC.
1971

The photogravure portrait of Herman Melville is now first reproduced from a photograph in the possession of Mrs. Henry K. Metcalf. The photograph was made in Pittsfield, Massachusetts in the early sixties, and the author's signature is reproduced from an autograph in the collection of Mr. Weaver.

Originally Published 1935
Published 1971 by Cooper Square Publishers, Inc.
59 Fourth Avenue, New York, N. Y. 10003
International Standard Book No. 0-8154-0383-6
Library of Congress Catalog Card No. 74-143858

Printed in the United States of America

INTRODUCTION

"With a philosophical flourish Cato throws himself upon his sword," Melville once wrote; "I quietly take to the ship. This is my substitute for pistol and ball."

Five times in his life, Melville took to the ship. And the first four of these, at least, were instigated in desperation.

It was as a lad of seventeen that Melville first set sail. "Sad disappointments in several plans which I had sketched for my future life," he says in *Redburn*, "the necessity of doing something for myself, united with a naturally roving disposition, conspired within me, to send me to sea as a sailor." Melville shipped on a merchantman bound for Liverpool. That was in 1837. And *Redburn*—published twelve years later—is the record of Melville's first hegira. "Talk not of the bitterness of middle-age . . . a boy can feel all that and much more, when upon his young soul the mildew has fallen. . . . And never again can such blights be made good . . . they strike too deep." In the words of Mr. H. S. Salt: "*Redburn* is a record of bitter experience and temporary disillusionment—the confessions of a poor, proud youth, who goes to sea 'with a devil in his heart' and is painfully initiated into the unforeseen hardships of a seafaring life."[1] It is a record, too, that Melville petulantly pretended to despise: "a thing which I, the author, know to be trash, and wrote it to buy some tobacco with."

[1] *The Bookman* (London), August, 1919. p. 165.

Melville's second "philosophical flourish" was extended in miles and protracted in years and is the basis of his fame. On January 3, 1841, he sailed from Fairhaven, in the whaler Acushnet, bound for the Pacific Ocean and the sperm whale fisheries. "Uppermost was the impression, that whatever swift, rushing thing I stood on was not so much bound to any haven ahead as rushing from all havens astern." It was a retreat from life, from reality and outward experience, from the world which has so early disappointed and blighted his soul. And the mood of this retreat is best indicated in the superb opening of *Moby-Dick:*

"Call me Ishmael. Some years ago—never mind how long precisely—having little or no money in my purse, and nothing particular to interest me on shore, I thought I would sail about a little and see the watery part of the world. It is a way I have of driving off the spleen, and regulating the circulation. Whenever I find myself growing grim about the mouth; whenever it is a damp drizzly November in my soul; whenever I find myself involuntarily pausing before coffin warehouses, and bringing up the rear of every funeral I meet; and especially whenever my hypos get such an upper hand of me, that it requires a strong moral principle to prevent me from deliberately stepping into the street, and methodically knocking people's hats off—then, I account it high time to get to sea as soon as I can. This is my substitute for pistol and ball."

From the tribal barbarities and smug provincialism of

New England to fifteen hideous months in the forecastle of a whaler; idyllic months among man-eating Epicures; mutiny off Tahiti; and service back home on board a man-of-war: all that, in Melville's own recounting in *Typee*, *Omoo* and *White-Jacket* is well known.

He returned to publish *Typee;* and in the first happy flush of incredulity at its success, he made two fatally mistaken choices: he married the charming daughter of a distinguished lawyer of Boston; he staked his livelihood on the making of books.

Typee had enjoyed a kind of refreshing *succès de scandale*—for here was a young writer from Polynesia who made first-hand and unflattering observations upon missionaries, and who in his unredemption had bathed with naked cannibal mermaids who smoked. *Typee* was followed rapidly by *Omoo*, and Victorian piety and lewdity were still piqued, as witness the effusion in *The American Review* 1847, Vol. VI. pp. 36-46, signed G. W. P. "He gets up voluptuous pictures, and with cool deliberate art breaks off always at the right point, so as without offending decency, he may stimulate curiosity and excite unchaste desire." Then, with the veiled and Orphic self-betrayals and the undigested exuberance of *Mardi*, came the rift. And with *Mardi* came likewise the dwindling of royalties. So Melville published *Redburn*. "Trash," he called it,[1] "written to buy some tobacco with," and the pronouncement is unamiable in its falsity. For in *Redburn* Melville had held the mirror up to him-

[1] *Journal of 1849*, November 6th.

self Narcissus-wise, and had made an unblushing ostentation of self-pity. In the midst of all of which, his wife was pregnant: and Melville was not only faced with the birth of a child, but with an account with his publisher overdrawn to the amount of $733.69.

The outlook at home was not bright. So for the third time, on October 11, 1849, Melville went down to the sea. *White-Jacket* he took with him in manuscript. He was bound a second time for England. And he had persuaded both his family and himself that he was heart-broken to depart. He smothered his guilty yearnings to get away under the assurance that, by personal intercession with English publishers, he could improve the income for home.

And while he was away, he kept the first journal of his that survives.

By the evidence of this journal (which has been published only in part)[1] he was torn between conflicting loyalties. But by the same evidence he did in vagabondage (well rationalized) steal much marginal and uncensured delight. He loved high and irresponsible talk for the mere and sufficient majesty it gave the diaphragm to expand,—and his relatives were not all metaphysicians. Too, he liked the Dionysian lift of potent liquids,—and though his mother descended from an august line of Dutch brewers, his immediate relatives rated worldly prosperity above ecstasy. Wives, babies, female relatives in adoring plenty, and relatives-by-marriage beside, he

[1]Chapter XIV of my *Herman Melville*.

had known in the dutiful plenitude of matrimony. Nowhere in his writings does he betray any particular pleasure in the intimacies of childbirth, but much repugnance rather: and he had recently presided over the completed rites of fatherhood. In the cradle of the deep, on the other hand, he was severed from all immediately challenging and hampering ties. So he conscientiously convinced all concerned that his carrying the manuscript of *White-Jacket* in person across the Atlantic was a gesture of self-sacrificing stoicism.

During the crossing he was expansively himself. There were those, of course, who came to see him off. He went aboard during a "cold violent storm from the West," and "as the ship dashed on, under double-reefed topsails, I walked the deck, thinking of what they might be doing at home." But, to his great delight, "I find myself in the individual occupancy of a large state-room—with a spacious berth, a large wash-stand, a sofa, glass, &c. &c. I am the only person on board who is thus honored with a room to himself. I have plenty of light, and a little thick glass window in the side. I have looked out upon the sea from it, often, tho not 24 hours on board." He played whist, he had a sound sleep, and he was "up betimes and aloft, to recall the old emotions of being at the mast-head." And he discovered many pleasant passengers aboard with whom to converse. Especially a Mr. Adler, with whom he walked the deck until a late hour, "talking of 'Fixed Fate, Free-will, free-knowledge absolute' &c. His philosophy is *Coleridgian;* he accepts the Scriptures as divine, and yet leaves himself free to inquire into Nature—he believes there are things not of God and independent of Him——" and before the following breakfast he was again up the mast-head. A crazy man jumped overboard and was drowned with a merry expression on his face. Melville was accosted by a friend of "Mr Twitchel who painted my portrait gratis"—and he grew to the amiable conviction that the passengers "seem to regard me as a hero" because of his feats in the rigging. Then he met a Dr. Taylor. "This afternoon Dr Taylor and I sketched a plan for going down the Danube from Vienne to Constantinople; thence to Athens on the steamer; to Beyroot and Jerusalem and Alexandria and the Pyramids."—"I am full (just now) of this glorious Eastern jaunt. Think of it:—Jerusalem and the Pyramids—Constantinople, the Aegean and also Athens!" Then he drank a bottle of stout, "and think it did me good."

And so, apparently, was first clearly sown in his mind the idea of the Journey up the Straits.

There followed an evening concert, and a delightful day. "Spent the entire morning in the main-top with Adler and Dr Taylor, discussing our plans for the grand circuit of Europe and the East." Then Taylor "communicated to me a circumstance that may prevent him from accompanying us—something of a pecuniary nature. He reckons our expense at $400." So, "after a hand at cards, retired."

On the morrow, he read an account of Venice in

Murray's guide-book, and "for the first time promenaded with some of the ladies." "In the evening for the first time went into the Ladies Saloon.—The saloon is guilt (sic) and brilliant, and as the ship was going on quietly, it seemed as if I were ashore in a little parlor or cabinet. Where's Orianna? Where's little Barney?"

This last would be unintelligible but for a pencil note in the margin inscribed by the initials of Melville's wife, E.S.M. Orianna, she tells us is "Lizzie"—that is, herself; Barney is "Macky"—that is, Malcolm their son. Melville concludes: "Towards morning was annoyed by a crying baby adjourning."

Then there were whiskey punches, and metaphysical sessions on Hegel and Kant until "after two in the morning." On a later evening, champagne, and on deck till midnight, and a rehearsal of the Eastern tour, which "renewed—at least in my mind—all my original enthusiasm. Talked the whole thing over with Taylor—Shall not be able to decide until we get to London."

Mulled wine, metaphysics and whist—and a parting at three A.M.—and on the following evening, "after claret and stout with Monsieur Moran and Taylor, went on deck and found it a moonlight midnight." On the evening following, "a superb dinner, which we relished amazingly."

"Just three weeks from home——"

"Get in tonight or tomorrow—or next week or year."

"This time tomorrow I shall be on land, and press English earth after the lapse of ten years—*then a sailor*, now H. M. author of 'Peedee,' 'Hullaboloo' and 'Pog-Dog.'"

And he concludes ashipboard with "Where dat old man?" In the margin, opposite this cryptic close, Melville's wife has written above her initials,—"First words of Baby Malcolm's."

Once ashore, it might seem, his enjoyment would not be quite so irresponsible. He saw publishers and picture galleries and the "sights," and bowed to Queen Victoria whose carriage passed him: "salute returned by the Queen but not by the Prince." He threw in the spectacle of a double execution before breakfast, and went much to the theatre when not soaring upon the verbiage of "metaphysics" or else "vagabonding thro' the courts and lanes and looking in at windows"; or else "went home, rigged up and jumped into an omnibus" to be lionized, and after gin, brandy, whiskey and cigars, "came away about 2 A.M. and through Oxford Street home and turned flukes"; or else "snooping about town to get a cheap dinner";—or else dined by his publisher Murray, to meet Lockhart "in a prodigious white cravat (made from Walter Scott's shroud, I suppose)"; or else "I hope to recover myself in the companionship and conversation of mortals.—'Oh, Solitude, where are thy charms'!" And nearly three weeks before his departure: "Tomorrow I am *homeward bound!* Hurrah and three cheers!"

Between times, he realized a hundred pounds on *Redburn,* and two hundred on *White-Jacket.* But his advances on royalties were inadequate for his projected jaunt to Constantinople. So he dropped for nine days into Paris and also viewed the Rhine.

In England, the Duke of Rutland had left his card. "It is now 3 P.M. I have had a fire made and am smoking a cigar. Would that one I knew were here. Would that the Little One too were here.—I am in a very painful state of uncertainty. I am all eagerness to get home—I ought to be home. My absence occasions uneasiness in quarters where I most beseech heaven to grant repose. Yet here I have before me an open prospect to get some curious idea of a style of life which in all probability I shall never have again. I should most like to know what the highest English aristocracy really and practically is—If I do not go, I am confident that hereafter I shall reprimand myself for neglecting such an opportunity of procuring 'material'—and Allan and others will account me a ninny."

Melville ended by deciding to deny himself this sacrifice of his family to his Art. So he wrote a refusal "and took a letter for a Duke to the post office and a pair of pants to be altered to a tailor."

This last was on December 18. Not until eight days later, however, did Melville finally and actually take ship pointing for home.

Ahead was the augmentation both of poverty and family ties; the agony of the creation of the masterpiece *Moby-Dick* and the hideousness of its public fiasco; the irony of the intemperate hope for some encouraging warmth of recognition from Hawthorne; and withal, threatened blindness and the collapse of his riotous good health. So with the publication of *Pierre*, Melville had to all appearance earned in the eyes of those whose waiting had been patient and faithful, his just reward as a shattered wreck and a used-up failure. Again he was ready for "pistol and ball."

The five years between the publication of *Moby-Dick* and his advent to the Holy Land were the most crucial in Melville's long life; and around these years hovers the lowering of the sinister intimation that his sanity was obscured. Before the publication of *Moby-Dick* lies the fecundity and precocity of his creativeness; and the thirty-four years ensuing upon his return from Jerusalem present no particular problem. During several seasons immediately after his "Voyage up the Straits" he was on the lecture platform; in May, 1860, he made a voyage to San Francisco, sailing from Boston on the thirtieth with his brother Thomas who commanded a fast sailing clipper in the China trade;[1] between December 5, 1866 and January 1, 1888, he was Inspector of Customs at the port of New York. In 1866 he published *Battle-Pieces and Aspects of the War;* with a Supplement, "gravely and well written, in which he counter-balances any Unionistic fervour and elation he might have shown in the battle poems, by discussing, with great sympathy and tact, the plight of the South and the psychological problems confronting the North, particularly, in dealing with it."[2] In 1876 appeared the 571 pages, two volumes, of

[1]The brief *Journal* of this was published in the *New England Quarterly* Vol. 2, No. 1—January, 1929.

[2]Lewis Mumford: *Herman Melville*, p. 303.

Clarel—A Poem and Pilgrimage in the Holy Land: in Four Parts; in his old age, two slight volumes of verse, privately printed, in editions of twenty-five copies. Unpublished, he left a bundle of scraps in prose and verse, and his swan-song, *Billy Budd,* all of which were published in the Constable edition of his works. Except for *Billy Budd,* all that he wrote after 1857 is, as achieved literature, negligible—though as a confession of the inner doubts and conviction, and the hidden conflicts in his heart during his long quietus, *Clarel* is invaluable; invaluable, too, as casting in retrospect much light into the dark places of his earlier turmoil.

It was Melville's particular misfortune that he was intimately entangled with a multitude of relatives not one of whom had any sympathetic understanding of him. Soon after Melville's return from the East, his cousin Henry Sanford Gansevoort reported: "Yesterday I visited Judge Shaw. I saw there Herman Melville. . . . Herman Melville seems considerably improved in health and spirits by his interspersing the spice of variety with the reality of life. I met him at Mr Griggs last Sunday evening. He was in a fine flow of humor which I enjoyed exceedingly. There is doubtless positive originality in him, Brilliance but misanthropy, Genius but less judgment. He evidently mistakes his sphere. He has dropped the pen of candid narrative for that of captious criticism. He does the latter well but he can do the former much better. I had the pleasure of listening to his lecture on Statuary in Rome delivered a week since. It was well conceived and executed but it lacked the force and beauty that characterise his early writing." Then follows a long digest of Melville's lecture. A week earlier, this same cousin had written to his father,—the uncle of Melville's, ironically, who paid for the publication of *Clarel:* "[Melville's] forte is narration or description in other words a wild, bold word painting—When he essays philosophy he seeks to ascend by waxen wings from his proper sphere only to find his mind dazzled his wings melted and his fall mortifying—" These letters appear in *The Family Correspondence of Herman Melville (1830-1904)*, edited in 1929 by Victor Hugo Paltsits, for the New York Public Library. Though the evidence of this *Family Correspondence* is scattered in time and slight in bulk, it is sufficient to redeem Melville from the charge of any obtrusive eccentricities in the everyday life of his latter years.

There survives, too, another, and an immensely personal document: the pocket diary of Melville's wife. It is a peculiarly intimate affair—the jottings of an old lady who has outlived her husband and her generation, and whose years have been crowded with tragic memories she was unable to understand and which she wished to efface. Eleven years after Melville's death she wrote in a letter: "My dear old pastor Dr Bellows used to quote to me the precept to 'Be faithful, and strengthen the things that remain.'" And that she did her best to accomplish. The pocket diary of her old age is slight in pages, recording the number of her watch and of her bankbook,—addresses of relatives and friends, and dates of births and deaths and marriages; a brief history of Arrowhead, and an inventory of legacies, and notes of furniture, plate, pictures, a blue quilted petticoat and an Empire gown. There is also, in two versions, the briefest biography of her dead husband. The latter half of the fuller version reads:

"Winters of 47 & 48 worked very hard at his books. Sat in a room without fire—wrapped up. Wrote Mardi—published ed. 1849. Summer of 1849 we remained in New York. He wrote Redburn & White Jacket. Same fall went to England & published the above. Staid 11 weeks. Took little satisfaction from it in mere homesickness & hurried home—leaving attractive invitations to visit various distinguished people—one from the Duke of Rutland to pass a week at Belvoir castle—see his Journal. We went to Pittsfield and boarded in the summer of 1850—moved to Arrowhead in fall October 1850. Wrote White Whale or Moby Dick under unfavorable circumstances—would sit at his desk all day not eating anything till four or five o'clock—then ride to the village after dark—would be up early and out walking before breakfast—sometimes splitting wood for exercise. Published White Whale in 1851—Wrote Pierre—published 1852. We all felt anxious about the strain on his health in spring of 1853. In 1854-5 & 6 wrote two books first published in seriels in Putnam's Monthly—and afterwards in book form—these were Israel Potter and the Encontadas—Also Piazza Tales some of which had previously appeared in magazines. In fall of 1856 he went to Europe and travelled 6 or 7 months going to the Holy Land. Came home about the time the Confidence Man was published in 1857—and with much improved health. In 13 years he had written 10 books besides much miscellaneous writing. He lectured in many parts of the country during the winters of '58, '59 & '60. In Feb 1855 he had his first attack of severe rhumatism in his back—so that he was helpless—and in the following June an attack of sciatica. Our neighbor in Pittsfield Dr. O, W. Holmes attended & prescribed for him. A severe attack of what he called crick in the back laid him up at his mothers in Gansevoort in March 1858—and he never regained his former vigor and strength."

Despite the meticulous precision of this gaunt digest so crowded with "facts," it reveals more about Mrs. Melville than of the subject it purports to treat. It is of Melville's achievements, and the handicap of his bodily ills. He had been a busy man, and he came to be a sick one. Such is Mrs. Melville's *apologia* for her husband. And the limitations of her piety and imagination that narrowed her vision to this, were, I believe, among the prime instigating causes to provoke in Melville the emotional crisis which she was pitiably unable to understand.

And that there was a crisis, between the publication of *Moby-Dick* and the journey to the Holy Land, is beyond debate. The sufficient evidence is in Melville's published work. Between 1851 (the date of *Moby-Dick*) and his return from the East in 1857, Melville published *Pierre, or The Ambiguities* (1852), *Israel Potter, His Fifty*

Kind of gallery, of marble, overlooking the entrance of the church; And here almost every day I would hang, looking down upon the spectacle of the scoffing Turks on the divan & the scowling pilgrims kissing the stone of the anointing. — The door of the church is like that of a jail — a grated wicket in it — The main body of the church is that covered by the ~~dome~~; a lofty & ruinous dome — ~~[illegible]~~ a sort of plague-stricken ~~dusty~~ splendor reigns ~~[illegible]~~ whose the fallen plastering reveals the meagre skeleton of beams & laths in the painted & mildewed walls around. ~~In the scribble~~

In the midst of all, stands the Sepulchre; a ~~[illegible]~~ church in a church. It ~~[illegible]~~ is of ~~[illegible]~~ marble, richly sculptured in parts & bearing the faded aspect of age. From its ~~[illegible]~~ ~~[illegible]~~ roof, ~~[illegible]~~ ~~[illegible]~~ hung a ~~[illegible]~~ garish ~~[illegible]~~ stream of lights upon the ~~[illegible]~~ faces of the pilgrims who crowd for admittance into a space which will hold but four or five at a time. You enter, ~~first~~ first passing a wee vestibule where is shown the stone on which the angel sat, you enter ~~[illegible]~~ the ~~[illegible]~~ tomb. ~~[illegible]~~ Wedged ~~[illegible]~~ ~~[illegible]~~ space, ~~[illegible]~~ the contracted ~~space, you are [illegible] by the [illegible], [illegible] the~~ It is like entering a lighted oven. ~~[illegible]~~ Wedged & half-stifled, you ~~[illegible]~~ stare for a moment on the ~~ineloquent~~ stone ineloquent of the Sepulchre slab, and glad to come out, ~~[illegible]~~ wipe your brow glad to escape ~~[illegible]~~ as from the heat & jam of a show-box. All is glitter & nothing is gold. A sickening cheat. The countenances of the poor & most ignorant pilgrims would tacitly seem to confess it as well as your own. After coming from the ~~Sepulchre,~~ they wander off listless, & sit down upon some of the many steps ~~...~~ After being but a little while in ~~the place,~~ the church, & then going the rounds of the other chapels & shrines, they either ~~...~~ stand still in listless ~~...~~ despondency, ~~...~~ or tear themselves in sealed ~~...~~ huddles about the minor stairways, ~~...~~ ~~...~~ indulging exchanges the sectarian gossip of the day. ~~...~~ The Church of the Sepulchre is the thronged news-room & sectarian & theological exchange of Jerusalem; ~~...~~ And well the name appears so, from the small little chapels ~~not bigger than the~~ the special property of the various sects of the Copts, the Syrians & others, which here & there catch the dim ~~...~~ near the eye, much like those ~~...~~ boxes of the stock-exchange, which one sees in other commercial exchanges. — — The Chapel of the Finding of the Cross. — wine cellar. &c.

— If you approach the church from the ~~...~~ squalid alley leading towards it from the Via Dolorosa, you pass a long, old ~~...~~ wall, lofty & dingy, in every corner of whose masonry lurks, or there are, ~~...~~ ~~...~~ lies in the sunshine an accumulation of the ~~...~~ vilest & least nameable filth of a city. (Turkish)
But at the time you are far from imagining that the wall treated with such apparent contumely (by the Turks, ...) is a main wall of the fabric containing the ~~...~~ tomb of ~~Christ.~~ God, one of the persons of the Godhead.

Years of Exile (1855), *The Piazza Tales* (1856), and *The Confidence Man: His Masquerade* (1857). *Moby-Dick* was dedicated to Nathaniel Hawthorne; *The Piazza Tales* is unique as being undedicated; *Israel Potter*, "To His Highness the Bunker-Hill Monument"; *The Confidence Man*, to a mountain—"To Greylock's Most Excellent Majesty."

Israel Potter is the life of a soldier of the Revolution, built upon *The Life and Remarkable Adventures of Israel R. Potter*. The copy in my possession is a pamphlet of 108 pages, printed in Providence in 1824, and priced at 28 cents. Besides this account, however, Melville leaned heavily upon a variety of other volumes, as has in detail been admirably established by Mr. W. Sprague Holden in a Master's Essay submitted at Columbia University in 1932. As for the novel itself, critics seem to be at odds about it. Mr. Percy Boynton calls it "a perfunctory work, not as interesting as the book it was based on." Mr. Lewis Mumford of course is convinced of "exactly the opposite,"—though he does allow that it "ranks far below Melville's best work." Mr. Frank Jewett Mather, Jr., finds in it "the best account of a sea-fight in American literature."[1] In any event it is a grim and ironic tale. And of its manner John Freeman remarked: "As if the attacks and sneers at his natural exuberance had indeed entered his soul, he resolved no more to cast his style to the swine but to restrict himself to the dry husks of language, putting an unnatural restraint upon his genius."

[1] *The Review*, Vol. 1, No. 14. August 16, 1919. p. 300.

—Then, as anticlimax: "In part this constraint brings benefit to the reader."[1]

As for the *Piazza Tales*, the critics of Melville seem for once in agreement upon the unevenness of the stories therein contained; and they seem to agree, again, that *Benito Cereno* (derived from Chapter XVIII of a book of voyages by Captain Amasa Delano, 1816)[2] and *The Encantadas* rank among the very finest of Melville's achievements as an artist. Sir Michael Sadleir, in his *Excursions in Victorian Bibliography*, in 1922 made the pioneer announcement that these stories "hold in the small compass of their beauty the essence of their author's supreme artistry." Since then, the drift of opinion has accorded with Sir Michael, and for once there has been amity in the Melville clan.

Not so, however, with *Pierre* and *The Confidence Man*. And on *Pierre* in especial have the critics of Melville split into diametrically opposing camps. By his own statement, it was not "supreme artistry" that absorbed the life and time of Melville in his writing of *Pierre*, "but the primitive elementizing of the strange stuff, which in the act of attempting that book, was upheaved and upgushed in his soul." Dr. Henry A. Murray concludes, in a beautifully keen and sober analysis of *Pierre:* "It is because in this instance Melville puts the soul of man first,

[1]*Herman Melville*, pp. 137-8.

[2]See the article by Harold H. Scudder in the *Publication of the Modern Language Association of America*, Vol. XVII. No. 2, June 1928.

and its literary shadowings-forth second that some critics consider *Pierre* his best book, and others consider it his worst."[1] Mr. E. L. Grant-Watson, for example, in a long dissertation on *Pierre*, pronounces it "the center of Melville's being, and the height of his achievement."[2] Unfortunately, those readers of Melville who do not share Mr. Grant-Watson's enthusiasm for upheavings and ungushings have not always in their dissent, been content to dismiss *Pierre*—and *The Confidence Man*—as being merely bad art. Some have further complicated matters by using these two books as sufficient basis to impugn Melville's sanity.

The most outspoken has been Mr. Julian Hawthorne. He charges: "As for the nightmare nonsense of *Pierre*, I was glad when it had gone down with the rest: it was the outcome of disease, distorted and repulsive: the sweet bells jangled out of tune and harsh."[3] A more formidable devil's advocate has risen in the person of Mr. Ludwig Lewisohn, who says: "Hawthorne had the power of creative self-catharsis, of projecting finished works—forever separate from his psyche—into the world. That gift Melville never attained. He fumed and fretted over the demon in his soul; he fled from it literally to the farthest isles of the sea; he hurled at it brief thunderbolts of sheer but intermittent genius; he sought to bury it under mountains of words. . . . The final image that arises

[1] *New England Quarterly*, Vol. IV, No. 2, April, 1931. p. 337.
[2] *Ibid*, Vol. III, No. 2, April, 1930. p. 232.
[3] *The Literary Digest International Book Review*, August, 1926. p. 561.

from all of Melville's work is that of a big bearded violently excited man trying to shout down the whimpering, lonely child in his soul."[1] Even with Mr. Lewisohn, however, there are distinctions of success and failure to be made among Melville's books; but he dismisses *Mardi* and *Pierre* as "mere phantasmagorias, clinical material rather than achieved literature." *The Confidence Man*, which appeared while Melville was away on his "Journey up the Straits," and which outdoes *Pierre* in *Pierre's* most perverse self-indulgences of the "spontaneous Me" is omitted by Mr. Lewisohn from the evidence of his damnation.

Mr. Lewis Mumford, however, who seems intent upon shedding a boundless sweet reasonableness upon all of Melville's works and days—even Mr. Mumford faced *The Confidence Man* not without qualifying misdoubts. "With Melville's actual life and predicament in mind, there are passages in *The Confidence Man* one cannot read without misgiving: the story of Charlemont, The Gentleman Madman, for one, and the story of the Man in Weeds, wedded to a fiendish woman, Goneril, who covers up her own lecherousness by attributing insanity to her husband. Likewise somewhat mysterious is the story of the Indian hater, who had been injured in youth by Indians, and never lost a chance to exterminate one. It is hard to fit these incidents into the logic of the plot; and their existence becomes plausible only if one believes Melville's own torments and suspicions had, for a

[1]*Expression in America*, pp. 186-9.

brief while, taken on a pathological character." This last, Mr. Mumford flatly refuses to believe. "The problem, though tantalizing," so Mr. Mumford urges, "is not of paramount importance; for there is plenty of independent evidence to show that by 1858 Melville had regained possession of himself, and that his further life, though full of hardship and difficulty, had nothing in it that placed him outside the pale of family life and friendship and decent social intercourse—although it may have been dogged by memories and revulsions from an earlier period, and by the continuation of evil suspicions in the minds of those to whom the normal abstentions and irritations that attend productive literary effort would themselves be an evidence of eccentricity, or something worse."

Mr. Julian Hawthorne dismisses Melville by the well-worn expediency of calling "morbid" and "crazy" anything that stirs up repugnance. The psychoanalysts have a name for this easy technique of exorcism. Mr. Lewisohn, on the other hand, demotes Melville as an artist: "No, Melville is not even a minor master. His works constitute rather one of the important curiosities of literature." But Mr. Lewisohn's is essentially a moral judgment. Mr. Mumford is a thoroughgoing fundamentalist and worships Melville as being a Supreme Master: "The day of Herman Melville's vision is now in the beginning. It hangs like a cloud over the horizon at dawn; and as the sun rises, it will become more radiant, and more a part of the living day": a pronouncement which is to me merely incomprehensible.

One certainty at least, however, stands clear and fixed in the midst of all this bad blood, and special pleading. And this certainty is: *Pierre* and *The Confidence Man* are not, by anybody's count, "achieved literature" in the transparent sense that that phrase applies to *Anna Karenina*, say, or *Hamlet*, or *Agamemnon*—works composed from the vantage ground of universal reason, above the passionate experience they body forth. Too rarely did Melville save his soul as an artist by losing it in something outside of himself.[1] Melville came to put the highest premium upon "sincerity," and the overwhelming bulk of his writing is "self-expression" and satire; the hero is always himself, either in his own undisguised person or else thinly masked in all sorts of romantic and allegorical finery. Since he was so much and so increasingly in earnest in his fiction, since he threw himself so unreservedly into his creations, since his imagination was so exclusively a vent for his personal preoccupations, rarely could he portray emotion, which demands detachment; usually he could but betray it. Withal, Melville did possess the power to stimulate, which is the beginning of greatness; and he had genius besides. But surely in *Pierre* and *The Confidence Man* he falls dizzily from being a writer of seasoned experi-

[1]See Mr. George Santayana's essay on "The Poetry of Barbarism" (*Religion and Poetry*). Though Mr. Santayana is concerned specifically with Whitman and Browning, and oblivious altogether of the existence of Melville, his essay is a brilliant analysis of Melville's limitations, both as an artist and as a thinker. The passage ensuing is evidence that I have admired this essay to the point of plagiarism.

ence and heavenly inspiration. And such a spectacular fall from grace must provoke in the spectator either embarrassment or else revulsion. Passion imperfectly transmuted into art can never inspire in a reader the serenity and the exultation of wonder; the reader is left rather with the disquietude of tensions unresolved, with an aching sense of unfulfillment, and a restless urge to do something about it: "to write a check or join a society," or to anatomize the faulty art as "clinical material." And, indeed, in one strict sense, a writer is good "clinical" material in direct proportion to the degree of his being a bad artist. And in this sense, as "clinical material," *Pierre* and *The Confidence Man* are of the best. And it is because Melville was throughout so uneven and undisciplined in his artistry, so chaotic in his miscellaneous exuberance, that most of his really attentive readers have been primarily interested in him as a tortured and cryptic personality. And upon the recklessness of his "sincerity" might be built up a whole series of psychoanalytical romances of the sort that Freud projected for da Vinci, or Mr. Joseph Wood Krutch for Poe. But never, except by the most unscrupulous abuse of language might even *Pierre* and *The Confidence Man* be invoked in proof that Melville was insane.

Unfortunately, there were those among Melville's immediate connections who understood him as remotely as did Julian Hawthorne. And it was precisely because of such misunderstandings that Melville was sent on the trip recorded in the *Journal* that follows. It is a fact that after *Moby-Dick* Melville's personal behavior grew even more perplexing to those who surrounded him. But fancy Michael Angelo so surrounded, or Dostoevsky, or Beethoven, and how similar would have been the perplexity! How their moods of taciturnity or their excitable outbursts would have occasioned a dumb solicitude or a blind distress irritating them to moments of murderous hatred! And the elegiacal family synods and the half-glances of accusing suspicion! So by 1856, when to the cousins and the sisters and the uncles and other of such like progeny, Melville seemed to be going from bad to worse—when he was a tired sick man hungry in his heart for some understanding companionship (which is one of the deepest and truest notes struck in *Clarel*); when his writings were earning him but a pittance; when the family both by marriage and by blood had tried in vain to get him a consular appointment to the Sandwich Islands or to any other remote place, or at best to do *something* for him; then, some one of them finally suggested in summary desperation: send him on a long trip, and pray for the rest.

Melville's father-in-law, Chief Justice Shaw subsidized the departure. And for the fourth time, on October 11, 1856, Melville set sail.

Family he left behind. Ahead was the Liverpool he had visited as a boy. Melville had himself tried for a consular appointment; and in Liverpool was the one man —who was in fact a consul—whom he had ever known who in his own person seemed to have realized all of

Melville's hopes, and the one man capable of envisioning the compass of Melville's apparent defeat.

Hawthorne entertained Melville at Southport upon his arrival, and in his *English Note-books*, under the date of November 20, has left the following account of his friend—which is not, incidentally, that of the mad-man his son has so fervidly imagined.

"A week ago last Monday, Herman Melville came to see me at the Consulate looking much as he used to do (a little paler, and perhaps a little sadder), a rough outside coat, and with his characteristic gravity and reserve of manner. He had crossed from New York to Glasgow in a screw steamer, about a fortnight before, and had since been seeing Edinburgh, and other interesting places. I felt rather awkward at first, because this is the first time I have met him since my ineffectual attempt to get him a consular appointment with General Pierce. However, I failed only from real lack of power to serve him; so there was no reason to be ashamed, and we soon found ourselves on pretty much our former terms of sociability and confidence. Melville has not been well of late; he had been afflicted with neuralgic complaints in his head and his limbs, and no doubt has suffered from too constant literary occupation, pursued without much success latterly; and his writings, for a long time past, have indicated a morbid state of mind. So he left his place at Pittsfield, and has established his wife and family, I believe, with his father-in-law in Boston, and is thus far on his way to Constantinople. I do not wonder that he found it necessary to take an airing through the world, after so many years of toilsome pen-labor following after so wild and adventurous a youth as his was. I invited him to come and stay with us at Southport as long as he might remain in this vicinity; and accordingly, he did come, on the next day, taking with him, by way of luggage, the least little bit of a bundle, which, he told me, contained a nightshirt and a toothbrush. He is a person of very gentlemanly instincts in every respect, save that he is a little heterodox in the matter of clean linen.

"He stayed with us from Tuesday till Thursday; and, on the intervening day, we took a pretty long walk together, and sat down in a hollow among sand-hills (sheltering ourselves from the high, cool wind) and smoked a cigar. Melville, as he always does, began to reason of Providence and futurity, and of everything that lies beyond human ken, and informed me that he had 'pretty much made up his mind to be annihilated'; but still he does not seem to rest in that anticipation, and, I think, will never rest until he gets hold of a definite belief. It is strange how he persists—and has persisted ever since I knew him, and probably long before—in wandering to and fro over these deserts, as dismal and monotonous as the sandhills amid which we were sitting. He can neither believe, nor be comfortable in his unbelief; and he is too honest and courageous not to try to do one or the other. If he were a religious man, he would be one of the most truly religious and reverential; he has a very high and noble nature and is better worth immortality than most of us.

"He went back with me to Liverpool on Thursday; and, the next day, Henry Bright met him at my office, and showed him whatever was worth seeing in town. On Saturday, Melville and I went to Chester; it being the one only place, within easy reach of Liverpool, which possesses any old English interest. . . . We left Chester at about four o'clock; and I took the rail for Southport at half-past six, parting from Melville at a street-corner in Liverpool, in the rainy evening. I saw him again on Monday, however. He said that he already felt better than in America; but observed that he did not anticipate much pleasure in his rambles, for the spirit of adventure is gone out of him. He certainly is much overshadowed since I saw him last; but I hope he will brighten as he goes onward. He sailed from Liverpool in a steamer on Tuesday, leaving his trunk behind him at my consulate, and taking only a carpet-bag to hold all his travelling gear. This is the next best thing to going naked; and as he wears his beard and moustache, and so needs no dressing case—nothing but a toothbrush—I do not know a more independent personage. He learned his travelling habits by drifting about, all over the South Seas, with no other clothes or equipage than a red flannel shirt and a pair of duck trousers. Yet we seldom see a man of less criticizable manners than he."

Seven years before, on the high seas, Melville had dreamed of Constantinople, Egypt, the Holy Land, and Greece. It was a chastened Melville who now, for the fourth time, sped from all havens behind.

INTRODUCTION

NOTE

Before I can let Melville speak for himself, a word is necessary about the text that follows.

This Journal is preserved in three volumes, all in the possession of Melville's grand-daughter, Mrs. Henry K. Metcalf. It would appear that Melville carried with him on this trip his Journal of 1849; for the account of his crossing is recorded on the few blank pages at the end of that book. The rest of the journal is in two volumes of fifty pages each, and of the size of the page herein produced in facsimile.

None of Melville's journals appeared in the Constable edition of his works: and for a very simple reason. This *Journal up the Straits*—as Melville called it—was in a handwriting that seemed to defy deciphering. When the Constable edition was proposed, already I had slaved over this *Journal* for two years; for the first half of it I had a text that at best was very tentative; for the second half I had a text as hopeless and as fragmentary as a papyrus frayed down the center and with every other word obliterated. Calvin Thomas, the Goethe scholar, who saw the *Journal*, said he had thought the manuscript of the second part of *Faust* was the worst in the world until he was convinced of what Melville could do.

At the top of one page Melville has this note in pencil: "Begun and continued at sea, which accounts for the part of the writing." This is too easy. In his writing, there is no consistency in the formation of the letters, which had the abiding tendency to reduce themselves to anonymous quavers. Nor is there even any assurance that there is any relation between the number of quavers and the number of letters in a word. He was a notoriously capricious speller, and so frequently the contortion on the page is but an impressionistic abbreviation into a short-hand that was all his own.

Two years ago, Mr. Gerald Crona called upon me, interested in Melville, and wanting to work on him towards a Master's Degree. As I look back upon it I see it was a cruel procedure: I put him to work on this Journal; and his text is the basis of mine.

My ideal has been to offer a perfect transcription of Melville's text, preserving all the peculiarities of his spelling and punctuation. There are, however, difficulties (besides human fallibility) that stand in way of such an attempt. To reproduce all his short-hand abbreviations and dropping of letters would be to caricature him into cypher; so such omissions I have always supplied, and I have always spelled the word correctly in all cases where the writing is ambiguous. The misspellings in my text are Melville's own.

Melville patently went back to this manuscript after his first writing of it, and the pages are decorated with pencil lines along the margins, and crosses in crayon, and rows of asterisks here and there between the lines, and passages underlined in pencil, and boxed, and encircled and crossed out. After his return, Melville drew repeatedly on the experiences of this trip, both in his lecture on "Statuary in Rome," and for a variety of writings which I have indicated in the notes to the text. But I cannot discover the remotest correspondence between his many markings and his later writings. So in my transcription I have disregarded these markings completely.

By the aid of maps, guide-books, encyclopedias, dictionaries biographical and otherwise, and the other resources of my own library and that of Columbia University, I have in every case (except where the contrary is indicated in the notes) confirmed my reading of Melville wherever it admitted of the possibility of confirmation. I might have appended notes, therefore, that in bulk would have obliterated the text. As it is, I have tried to reduce the notes to the minimum I have judged necessary to clarifying the text without burdening it.

Besides my indebtedness to Mr. Crona, I owe unique thanks, of course, to Mrs. Henry K. Metcalf. To name all those who have generously responded to my requests for help would be to give an enumeration of all of my friends as well as of a score of strangers and specialists whose aid I have invoked. But there are three in particular who have helped me most: my friends and colleagues Harry K. Dick, Dorothy Brewster, and John Angus Burrell.

RAYMOND WEAVER

JOURNAL

Conversations with the Colonel on fixed fate &c. during the passage[1]

Sailed from New York Oct. 11th, Saturday, 1856 in the screw-steamer Glasglow bound for Glasglow. In 15 days made the north of Ireland,—Rathlin isle—passed Arran, Ailsa Crag &c (see map). Ailsa looming up in the mist. Got to Greenoch 10 at night, lay there at anchor, next morning, Sunday, went up the Clyde to Glasglow. Great excitement all along. Banks like tow-paths—narrow channel — immense steamer — green heights — received by acclamation—Lord Blantyre's place—

[1]In Melville's manuscript, this entry occupies a page to itself. The ancient debate over the freedom of the will seems to have been an especially live and abiding question to Melville. His *Clarel: A Poem and Pilgrimage in the Holy Land* (the two volumes of which are based upon experiences recorded in these journals which follow), begins its dedication with the phrase "By a spontaneous act." This concern of Melville's (which might be much more fully elaborated) over "fixed fate" and "spontaneous acts" parallels André Gide's absorption with "*l'act gratuit.*" (*Vide* Léon Pierre-quint's *André Gide*, Paris, 1932).

opposite mud cottage—cattle tenders—women—face like cattle—places for building iron steamers.

Next morning went to old cathedral,—tombs, defaced inscriptions—others worn in flagging—some letters traced in moss—back of cathedral gorge & stream—Acropolis—John Knox in Geneva cap frowning down on the cathedral—dimness of atmosphere in keeping—all looked like picture of one of the old masters smoked by Time—

Old buildings about the hill, stone walls & thatch roof—solid & fragile—miserable poverty—look of the middle ages—west end & fine houses—the moderns—contemporary.—The University. The park—the promenade (Seychill[1] street)—at night population in the middle of the street. High Street. *Next morning* took steamer down the Clyde to Loch Lomond—R.R. part of the way—thick mist, just saw the outline of Ben Lomond—like lake George—came back & stopped at Dumbarton Castle—isolated rock, like Ailsa—promontory at the juncture of the Clyde & Levern[2]—covered with sod & moss—a cleft between—stone stairs & terraces—W. Wallace's broadsword—great cleaver—soldiers in red coats about the Rock like flamingoes among the cliffs—some rams with smoky fleeces—grene-

[1]Melville's spelling for Sauchiehall?

[2]Leven.

diers—smoked by the high chimneys of furnaces in Dumbarton village—

Continued in small mem. book marked "Journal up the Straits". Sailed from Liverpool to Constantinople Nov. 18—1856.[1]

Memorandum of stay in Liverpool

Begun and continued at sea, which accounts for the part of the writing[2]

Saturday, Nov 8th 1856. Arrived from York, through Lancaster, at 1 P. M., having passed through an interesting country of manufactures. A rainy day. Put up at "White Bear Hotel" Dale St:. Dined there at ordinary. Before sitting down, asked barmaid, "How much?" Curious to observe the

[1]In pencil, so faint as to be barely legible.
[2]In pencil.

shrinking expression, as if shocked at the idea of anything mercenary having part in the pure hospitality of an ordinary. Host & hostess at table. Comical affectation of a private dinner party. All thought of the public house banished. Entertaining his friends. "Will you have some ale?"—But charged in the bill.—Affectation of the unstinted bounty of a Christmas party, but great economy.—Capital bed.—After dinner went to Exchange. Looked at Nelson's statue, with peculiar emotion, mindful of 20 years ago.[1]—Stayed at hotel during the evening. Rain. Made acquaintance with an agreeable young Scotchman going to the East in steamer "Damascus" on Monday. Wanted me to accompany him. Sorry that circumstances prevented me.

Sunday, Nov. 9th Rain. Stayed home till dinner. After dinner took steamboat for Rock Ferry to find Mr Hawthorne. On getting to R.F., learned he had removed thence 18 months previous, & was residing out of town.—Spent evening at home.

Monday Nov 10th Went among docks to see the Mediterranean steamers. Explored the new docks "Huskisson" &c. Saw Mr Hawthorne at the Consulate. Invited me to stay with him during my

[1]See *Redburn*, 196 ff. (This, as all other citations from Melville's published works, is from the Constable Edition, London, 1922-1924.)

sojourn at Liverpool.—Dined at "Anderson's" a very nice place, & charges moderate.

Tuesday Nov 11 Went among the steamers in the morning. Took afternoon train with Mr Hawthorne for Southport, 20 miles distant on the seashore, a watering place. Found Mrs. Hawthorne & the rest awaiting tea for us.

Wednesday Nov 12 At Southport. An agreeable day. Took a long walk by the sea. Sands & grass. Wild & desolate. A strong wind. Good talk.[1] In the evening Stout & Fox & Geese.—Julian grown into a fine lad; Una taller than her mother. Mrs Hawthorne not in good health. Mr H. stayed home for me.

Thursday Nov 13. At Southport till noon. Mr H. & I took train then for Liverpool. Spent rest of day pressing inquiries among steamers, & writing letters, & addressing papers &c.

Friday Nov 14—Took 'buss for London Road,—"Old Swan" Passed ———.[2] Returning, called at Mr Hawthornes. Met a Mr Bright.[3] Took me to his Club & lunched there. Then to view Unitarian church, & Free Library & Cemetery.

[1]Hawthorne's account of this afternoon is quoted at length in the Introduction.

[2]Undecipherable.

[3]Henry A. Bright, who, according to Julian Hawthorne's biography of his parents (Vol. II, p. 21) "had been introduced to Hawthorne in Concord, by Emerson, in the autumn

Saturday Nov 15 Rode in the omnibus. Went out to Toxteth Park &c—Grand organ at St. George's Hall.
Sunday Nov 16 In the morning packed trunk. To church in the afternoon, & evening.
Monday Nov 17 Was to sail to day in "Egyptian" Captain Tate, but put off till tomorrow. Great disappointment. Tired of Liverpool.
Tuesday Nov 18—Sailed about three o'clock. Fine sight going out of harbor.

Voyage from Liverpool to Constantinople

Nov 19th. Saw Tusca[1] Rock, on Irish Coast.
Nov 20, 21, 22d Fair wind & fine weather. Passed Cape Finisterre.
Sunday 23d. Passed within a third of a mile of Cape St: Vincent. Light house & monastery on bold cliff. Cross. Cave underneath light house. The whole Atlantic breaks here. Lovely afternoon.

of 1852, and who came to be perhaps the most intimate of his English friends." After Hawthorne's death Longfellow wrote Bright: "I am glad to know how deeply you feel this loss; for I know, having heard it from his own lips, that he liked you more than any man in England."

[1]Melville's spelling for Tuskar.

Great procession of ships bound to Crimea must have been descried from this point.

Monday 24th Strong wind ahead. Sighted Cape Trafalgar. Entered the Strait of Gibraltar at 4. P.M. Mountainous & wild-looking coast of Africa—forsaken barbarous, "Apes Mountains" nearly opposite Gibraltar. "Pillars of Hercules." Tarifa, small village,—white. Insular Rock. Sunset. Rock strongly lit, all the rest in shade. England throwing the rest of the world in shade. Vast heigth. Red sky. Sunset in the Straights. Gate of the East. Many ships.—Looks insular as Bass Rock or Ailsa.—Calm within Straits. Long swell took us. The Mediterranean.

Tuesday 25. Nov. Beautiful morning. Blue sea & sky. Warm as May. Spanish coast in sight. Mountains, snow capped. always so Captain says. Mate came out with straw hat. Shirt sleeves. Threw open my coat.—Such weather as one might have in Paradise. Pacific. November too! Like sailing on a lake.

Wednesday 26. At sunrise close to African Coast. Mountains, in parts crested with snow. Peeps of villages. Wild looking. At noon, off Algiers. In the vicinity beautiful residences among the hills. White house among gardens. Reminded one of passages in Don Quixotte, "Story of the Morisco." Saw the mole & light house—the town[1] built up a hill—

[1]Questionable reading.

latteen boats in view. The sun hot. High mountains all around. Fine bay. Piratical corsair look. —Leaving it in the distance the town looked like a sloping rock, covered with bird lime—the houses all white.—In the afternoon passed a detached group of very high mountains covered a long way down with snow—Alpine heigths . . The most solitary & dreariest imaginable.

Thursday 27th Same glorious weather. In the evening passed Isle Galeta — uninhabited. Clear nights, stars shining with brilliancy.

Friday 29th.[1] Bright & blue as usual. At noon passed close to Pantalaria,[2] an isle 150 ms from Malta, & 200 from Africa. Cultivated slopes & plains all round a mass of lofty rock. Beautiful landscapes inland. A town & scattered houses. A large castle. Belongs to Naples. Convicts here.—Went to bed at 8. P. M and at 1. A. M. dressed & went on deck, the ship about entering Malta harbor. To bed again when anchor was down.

Saturday, 29th Lying in the harbor of Malta. Ashore all day. At 6. P. M. got under weigh, with two passangers in cabin, a Greek & Austrian, very gentlemanly men.

Sunday 30 Cross sea, ship rolling very bad. G & A

[1]Above the line is written: *one day error in date.*
[2]Pantelleria.

quite sick. Rather dismal day. At night had to secure myself in berth against being rolled out.
Monday Dec 1 Sea less cross. At 12. M. pleasant, & made the coast of Greece, the Morea. Passed through the straits, & Cape Matapan.
Tuesday Dec 2. At daylight in the midst of Archipelago; 12 or 15 islands about. Came to anchor at Syra about 8 A. M. Port of the Archipelago. Much alarmed lest we should have a quarantine of eleven days. Saw the quarantine house—lonely place among bare hills; opposite the shipping. At the custom house with the Captain & his papers; at a grating, took the ship's papers with pair of wooden tongs. Meantime an officer off to the ship to muster the crew; if one man dead, or missing,—quarantine! All right, though.—Went ashore. New & old Town. Animated appearance of the quay. Take all the actors of opera in a night from the theatres of London, & set them to work in their fancy dresses, weighing bales, counting codfish, sitting at tables on the dock, smoking, talking, sauntering,—sitting in boats &c—picking up rags, carrying water casks, lemonade &c—will give some notion of Greek port. Picturesqueness of the whole. Variety of it. Greek trousers, sort of cross between petticoat & pantaloons. Some with white petticoats & embroidered jackets. Fine forms,

noble faces. Mustache &c.—Went to Old Town. From the water looks like colossal sugarloaf. White houses. Divided from New Town by open lots. Climbed up. Complete warren of stone houses or rather huts, built without the least plan, zig-zag. little corrals in front of each, sometimes overhead, crossing the track. Paved with stone, roofs flat & m'cadamed. Up & up, only guide was *to mount*. At last got to the top, a church, from court of which, fine view of archipelago & islands (name them)— Looks very old;—probably place of defence. Poor people live here. Picturesque. Some old men looked like Pericles reduced to a chiffonier[1]—such a union of picturesque & poverty stricken.—Streets of stairs up the Old Town. As if made for goats. The donkeys climb them. All round barren tawny hills, here & there terraced with stone. Saw a man ploughing with a piece of old root.—Some roofs plaited. Very dirty. Terrible nest for the plague.—View of the islands—little hamlets, white, half way up mountains.—The azure of the sea, & ermine of the clouds, the Greek flag (blue & white) seems suggested by the azure of her sky & ermine of her clouds.

The wharf, a kind of semicircle, coinciding with

[1]Melville seems to have had a weakness for this word. It is from the French *chiffon*, meaning a rag.

the amphitheatre of hills.—In December tables & chairs out of doors, coffee & water pipes.—Carpenters & blacksmiths working in the theatrical costumes.—Scavenger in his opera costume going about with dust pan & brush, & emptying his pan into panniers of an ass.—No horses or carriages—streets merely made for footpassengers. — The crowds on the quays all with red caps, looking like flamingoes. Long tassells—laborers wear them, & carry great bundles of codfish on their heads.—Few seem to have anything to do. All lounge. Greek signs over a pieman's.[1]

Wednesday & Thursday 3d & 4th Still at Syra. On the last day I did not go ashore. Several steamers arrived. Got my sovereigns back from Loyd's. Other two passengers sailed for Athens.

Friday 5th At 2 A. M got under weigh for Salonica. Passed various islands. First bad weather encountered since leaving England. Rain & wind. About sunset passed through very narrow passage into the Gulf of Salonica. In the cabin had a Greek gentleman & wife for passengers; with 12 or 15 Greeks for deck passengers. Steamed slowly during the night, so as to make the harbor at a proper time in the morning.

[1]Cf. this account—and that of the two other times he touched at Syra—with the poem *Syra* (*A Transmitted Reminiscence*)—*Timoleon* 289 ff.

Saturday 6th At day break roused by the Captain to come on deck. Did so. Saw Mount Olympus, covered with snow at the summit, & looking most majestic in the dawn. Ossa & Pelion to the South. Olympus 10,000 feet high, according to the Captain's chart. O. & P. about 4 or 5000. Long ranges of hills along the Thessalonian shore. Mount Athos (rather conical) on the opposite shore. About nine o'clock came to anchor before Salonica. A walled town on a hill side. Wall built by Genoese. Minarets & cypress trees the most conspicuous objects. Two Turkish men of war in harbor. Olympus over against the town far across the water, in plain sight. Went with Captain with papers to the quarantine. All right & shook hands. (Usual ceremony of welcome). Went to the Abbots, ship's agents. Politely received. One of their employees took me a strole through the town. Went into the mosques. Tomb of an old Greek saint shown in a cellar. Several of the mosques formerly Greek churches, but upon the conquest of the Turks turned into their present character. One of them circular & of immense strength. The ceiling mosaic. Glass. Pieces continually falling upon the floor. Brought away several.[1]—Saw Roman remains of a triumphal arch across a street. Fine sculpture at the

[1]Still surviving among Melville's effects.

base representing battle scenes. Roman eagle conspicuous. About the arch, miserable buildings of wood. A Turkish cafe near one pier. Also saw remains of a noble Greek edifice. 3 columns &c. used as gateway & support to outhouse of a Jew's abode. Went into the Bazaar. Quite large, but filthy. Streets all narrow, like cow lanes, & smelling like barn-yards. Very silent. Women muffled about the face. All old. No young. Great numbers of Jews walking in long robes & pelisses. Also Greeks mixed with the Turks. Aspect of streets like those of Five Points.[1] Rotten houses. Smell of rotten wood. Three months ago a great fire, overrunning several acres. Not yet rebuilt. 60 persons killed by explosion of powder in a Greek warehouse,—powder not known to have been there.

Sunday Dec 7th Purposed going with Captain Tate to the Protestant missionaries, but learned they

[1]Slum district in old New York City, formed by the intersection of Cross, Anthony, Little Water, Orange, and Mulberry streets. These debouched into a triangular area almost an acre in extent, in the center of which was a small park called Paradise Square, surrounded by a fence which used to serve as the community clothes line. Dancing was the chief diversion of the district, as were the Hot Corn Girls. By 1840 Five Points was notorious as the most dismal slum section in America. Dickens devotes some highly colored paragraphs to it in his *American Notes*. See Herbert Asbury, *The Gangs of New York*, 5 ff.—

were absent at Cassandra. Duckworth, the English resident, came off early. Talked with him. Said he had been *a day's shooting in the Vale of Tempe*[1]—Ye Gods! whortleberrying on Olympus, &c.—Went ashore with Captain. Started for Abbots' on horseback with a guide & guard to the Abbotts place three miles inland. On emerging from gate met the first troop of camels. Passed an immense cemetery. Turbanded tombstones. Rode over bleak hills—no verdure—here & there an old sycamore. A shade with fountain, & inscription from the Koran. Passed some vineyards. Abbots place enclosed by high thick stone wall. On knocking, after a good time, gate was opened, & we were repulsed. But presented letter. Guards came running with muskets. Letter read at last by a handsome, polite Greek, who then led us through the grounds. Oriental style. Very beautiful. Hot houses & fountains & trellises & arbors innumerable. Old sycamores. Served with sweet-meats & liquers & coffee. Bath rooms. Thick dome perforated — light but no heat. — Returned at 3 P. M. & dined aboard.—Saw several flocks of sheep & shepherds on the hills. Met donkeys a plenty.

[1]Cf *Clarel* Vol. 1, p. 193:
"Fine shot was mine by Nazareth;
But birding's best in Tempe's Vale:"

Surprising loads they carry. Long timbers, bales &c. Scene in the Gate.—In the evening Captain told a story about the heat of arms affecting the compass.[1]

Beautiful weather all day, & gloriously clear night.

Monday Dec 8th Lovely day. Ashore & visited the walls. Was repulsed from a tower by a soldier who refused money. Went through the bazars. At the landing watched for an hour or two a vast crowd & tourist.[2] An Austrian steamer from Constantinople just in, with a great host of poor deck passengers, Turks, Greeks, Jews &c. Came ashore in boats, piled up with old dusty traps from which the Plague seemed shaken. Great uproar of the porters & contention for luggage.—Imagine an immense accumulation of the rags of all nations, & all colors rained down on a dense mob, all struggling for huge bales & bundles of rags, gesturing with all gestures & wrangling in all tongues. Splashing into the water from the grounded boats. —After dinner on board, several deck passengers came off to us to go to Constantinople. Turkish women among others. Went right aft on deck & spread their carpets. One prayed, bowing her head.

[1]It would seem that *The Timoneer's Story* (*Clarel*, Vol. 2, 58 ff.) had its genesis in this story of Captain Tate's.

[2]Questionable reading.

Two negresses, faces covered, to conceal their beauty. Arms all taken down into the cabin after being discharged:—(Captain T's story of arms)[1]—Upon the uproar at the landing Olympus looked from afar cold & snowy. Surprising the Gods took no interest in the thing. Might at least have moved their sympathy.—Heard a rumor by way of Trieste that Louis Napoleon had been assassinated.[2]—Forgot to mention the pulpit of St. Paul in the court of a mosque. Beautiful sculpture—all one stone. Steps &c. The chief lion of Salonica, is this.

Tuesday Dec 9th Remained on board, observing the arrival of deck passengers for Constantinople. A large number in all costumes. Among others two "beys effendi" in long furred robes of yellow, looking like Tom cats. They had their harems with them. All on deck. At 1½ P. M got under weigh. Lovely day. A calm. Ship steady as a house. Like a day in May. A moonlight night followed. Passed Olympus glittering at top with ice. When it was far astern, its snow line showed in the moonlight like a strip of white cloud. Looked unreal—but still was there. Passed Ossa & Pelion. Rounded Athos. Got up tents for the two harems. Guard set

[1]In pencil, above the line.

[2]The rumor was premature. On Jan. 14, 1858 Orsini made an unsuccessful attempt upon his life. He lived till 1873.

over them. Fine old effendi wounded at Sinope. Some very pretty women of the harem. "Ashmacks"[1] worn by them. Very lazy.

Wednesday Dec 10th. Up early, fine morning, off "Lemnos, the Ægean isle". Passed to the north of it, between it & Imbros. About 11 A. M. entered the Helespont. Gentle wind from the north. Clear & fine. The new castles of Europe & Asia on either hand. Little difference in the aspect of the continents. (For Asia here see 2d book—Zion)[2]. Only Asia looked a sort of used up—superannuated. Shores moderately lofty. A sober yellow the prevalent colour. Passed a good many vessels bound down before a gentle wind with all sail set. Among others a Turkish steam friggate. Passed the new castles at the Dardenelles proper; then Point Nagara; then Cape Sestos & Abydos—a long swim had Leander & Byron; then Gallipoli, where the French & English first landed during the War. Then entered the Sea of Marmora, where we were suddenly met by a dense fog. It cleared up soon

[1]"The Yashmak, you know, is not a mere semi-transparent veil, but rather a good substantial petticoat applied to the face; it thoroughly conceals all the features except the eyes; the way of withdrawing it is by pulling it down." Kinglake's *Eōthen*, note on p. 26, of the anonymous edition published by George P. Putman, New York, 1849.

[2]In pencil, between the lines.

however; but was followed by other mists. The weather changed.—The sail up the Helespont is upon the whole a very fine one. But I could not get up much enthusiasm; though passing Xerxes' bridge-piers (or the site of them) & the mouth of the Granicus, &c &c &c. Still, I thought what a sublime approach has the Sultan to his Capital. Antechambers of seas & lakes, & corridors of glorious straits. *8½ P. M.* Tomorrow morning I must rise betimes to behold Constantinople, where it remains to be seen how long I shall sojourn. N.B. Cap. T. has not yet accounted for the piastres. *Thursday Dec 11th* Thick fog during the night. Steamed very slowly, ringing the bell. Ere daylight came to anchor in the Sea of Marmora, as near as the Captain could determine, within but three miles or less of Constantinople. All day the fog held on. Very thick, & damp & raw. Very miserable for the Turks & their harems; particularly when they were drowned out by the deck-washing. Some sick & came below to the fire; off with the "ashmacks" &c. Several steamers at anchor around us, but invisible; heard the scream (alarms) of their pipes & ringing of bells.—During the second night heard the Constantinople dogs bark & bells ring. Old Turk ("Old Sinope") I said to him "This is very bad" he answered "God's will is good, & smoked his pipe in cheerful resignation. *Friday Dec 12th.* About noon fog slowly cleared away before a gentle breeze. At last, as it opened around us, we found ourselves lying, as in enchantment, among the Princes Islands, scores of vessels in our own predicament around us. Jumble confounded.[1] (Forgot to note that during the fog several "kyacks" came alongside, attracted by our bell. They had lost their way in the fog. They were Constantinople boats. One of them owned by a boy, who moored under our quarter & there went to sleep in the fog. Specimen of an Oriental news boy. The self-possession & easy ways. The first appearance of Constantinople from the sea is described as magnificent. See "Anastasius"[2] But we lost this. The fog only lifted from about the skirts of the city, which being built upon a promontory, left the crown of it hidden wrapped in vapor. Could see the base & wall of St. Sophia but not

[1]The reading of this sentence is uncertain; the script here is especially tantalizing.

[2]A novel by Thomas Hope (1770-1831). To his journal of his trip abroad in 1849, Melville appended a list of the books he brought back with him. From Bentley he got a 2 Vol. edition of "Anastasius"; in Paris he bought a second copy for "about 4 francs." Of this copy Melville says in his 1849 Journal under the date of Thursday 13th December: "Breakfasted, & took myself off to the Customs House to get my

the dome. It was a coy disclosure, a kind of coquetting, leaving room for imagination & heightening the scene. Constantinople, like her Sultanas, was thus seen veiled in her "ashmack". Magic effect of the lifting up of the fog disclosing such a city as Constantinople.—At last rounded Seraglio Point & came to anchor at 2 P M on the Golden Horn. Crossed over to Tophanna in a caique (like a canoe, but one end pointed out like a knife, covered with quaint carving, like old furniture). No demand made for passport nor any examination of luggage. Got a guide to Hotel du Globe in Pera. Wandered about a little before dinner. Dined at 6 P. M. 10 F per day for 5th story room without a carpet &c. Staid in all night. Dangerous going out, owing to footpads & assassins. The curse of these places. Can't go out at night, & no places to go to, if you could. Burnt districts.

Saturday Dec 13th. Up early; went out; saw cem-

luggage thro'. They seized my fine copy of 'Anastasius' & told me it was food for fine. Was much enraged thereat." Thomas Hope was an unusually picturesque character; and his "Memoirs of a Greek," published anonymously in 1819, was first generally attributed to Lord Byron, who told Lady Blessington that for two reasons he wept bitterly on reading it: because he had not written it, and because Hope had. Melville here refers to the last paragraph of Chapter Three: too long to quote.

eteries, where they dumped garbage. Sawing wood over a tomb. Forrests of cemeteries. Intricacy of the streets. Started alone for Constantinople and after a terrible long walk, found myself back where I started. Just like getting lost in a wood. No plan to streets. Pocket compass. Perfect labyrinth. Narrow. Close, shut in. If one could but get *up*. Aloft, it would be easy to see one's way out. If you could get up into tree. Soar out of the maze. But no. No names to the streets no more than to natural allies among the groves. No numbers. No anything.— Breakfast at 10 A. M. Took guide ($1.25 per day) and started for a tour. Took caique for Seraglio. Holy ground. Crossed some extensive grounds & gardens. Fine buildings of the Saracenic style. Saw the mosque of St Sophia. Went in. Rascally priests demanding "bakshish". Fleeced me out of ½ dollar; following me round, selling the fallen mosaics.[1] Ascended a kind of horse way leading up, round & round. Came out into a gallery fifty feet above the floor. Superb interior. Precious marbles, Porphyry & verd antique. Immense magnitude of the building. Names of the prophets in great letters. Roman Catholic air to the whole.—

To the Hippodrome, near which stands the six towered mosque of Sultan Achmet; soaring up with

[1]Still preserved among Melville's effects.

its snowy spires into the pure blue sky (like light-houses.)[1] Nothing finer. In the hippodrome saw the obelisk with Roman inscriptions upon the base. Also a broken monument of bronze, representing three twisted serpents erect upon their tails. Heads broken off. Also a square monument of masoned blocks. Leaning over & frittered away—like an old chimney stack. A Greek inscription shows it to (be)[2] of the time of Theodosius. Sculpture about the base of the obelisk, representing Constantine, wife & sons, &c. Then saw the "Burnt Column". Black & grimy enough & hooped about with iron. Stands soaring up from among a huddle of old wooden rookeries. A more striking fire monument than that of London. Then to the Cistern of 1001 columns. You see a rounded knoll covered with close herbage. Then a kind of broken cellar way, you go down, & find yourself on a wooden, rickety platform, looking down into a grove of marble pillars, fading away into utter darkness. A palatial sort of Tartarus. Two tiers of pillars one standing on t'other; lower tier half buried. Here & there a little light percolates through from breaks in the keys of the arches; where bits of green straggle down. Used to be a reservoir. Now full of boys

[1]In pencil, between the lines.
[2]Melville omitted the verb.

twisting silk. Great hubbub. Flit about like imps. Whir of the spinning jennies. In going down, (as into a ship's hold) and wandering about, have to beware the innumerable skeins of silk. Terrible place to be robbed or murdered in. At whatever point you look, you see lines of pillars, like trees in an orchard arranged in the quincunx style.—Came out. Overhead looks like a mere shabby common, or worn out sheep pasture.—To the Bazarr. A wilderness of traffic. Furniture, arms, silks, confectionery, shoes, saddles—everything. (Cairo.)[1] Covered overhead with stone arches, with side openings. Immense crowds. Georgians, Armenians, Greeks, Jews & Turks are the merchants. Magnificent embroidered silks & gilt sabres &. Caparisons for horses. You loose yourself & are bewildered & confounded with the labyrinth, the din, the barbaric confusion of the whole.—Went to the Watch Tower within a kind of arsenal. (immense arsenal.) The Tower of vast girth & heigth in the Saracenic style—a column. From the top, my God, what a view! Surpasses everything. The Propontis, the Bosphorus, the Golden Horn, the domes, the minarets, the bridges, the men of war, the cypresses.—Indescribable.—Went to the Pigeon Mosque. In its courts, the pigeons covered the

[1]In pencil, in the right margin.

pavement as thick as in the West they fly in hosts. A man feeding them. Some perched upon the roof of the collonades, & upon the fountain in the middle & on the cypresses.—Took of my shoes, & went in. Pigeons inside, flying round in the dome, in & out the lofty windows.—Went to Mosque of Sultan Sulyman. The third one in point of size & splendor.—The Mosque is a sort of marble marquee of which the minarets (four or six) are the stakes. In fact when inside it struck me that the idea of this kind of edifice was borrowed from the tent. Though it would make a noble ball room.—Off shoes & went in. This custom more sensible than taking off hat. Muddy shoes; but never muddy heads. Floor covered with mats & over them beautiful rugs of great size & square. Fine light coming through side slits below the dome. Blind dome. Many Turks at prayer; bowing head to the floor towards a kind of altar. Chanting going on. In a gallery saw a lot of portmanteaux chests & bags; as in a R.R. baggage car, put there for safe-keeping by men who leave home, or afraid of robbers & taxation. "Lay not up your treasures where moth & rust do corrupt" &c. Fountains (a row of them) outside along the sides of the mosque for bathing the feet & hands of worshippers before going in. Natural rock.—Instead of going in in stockings (as I did) the Turks wear over shoes & doff them outside the mosque.—The tent like form of the mosque broken up & diversified with infinite number of arches, buttresses,[1] small domes, collonades, cupolas &c &c &c.—Went down to Golden Horn. Crossed bridge of pontoons. Stood in the middle & not a cloud in the sky. Deep blue & clear. (Sultan's ships in colors—no atmosphere like this for flags.)[2] Delightful elastic atmosphere, altho December. A kind of English June, cooled & tempered sherbert-like with an American October; the serenity & beauty of summer without the heat. (No wonder poor homes. Don't want them. Open air. Chairs in the streets—crowds &c.)[2]—Came home through the vast suburbs of Galata &c. Great crowds of all nations—money changers—coins of all nations circulate—Placards in four or five languages; [(Turkish, French, Greek, Armenian.) Lottery] advertisements of boats the same. You feel you are among the nations. Great curse that of Babel; not being[3] able to talk to a fellow being, &c.—Have to beware of your pockets. My guide

[1]In pencil, above the line, and boxed, is written: *Begin here.*

[2]Written vertically along the left margin.

[3]The page ends here. At the bottom, faintly in pencil, is written: *I feel among the nations.* At the top of the following page, underscored and in ink: (*Ruffians of Galata*).

went with his hands in his.—The horrible grimy tragic air of the streets. The rotten & wicked looking houses. So gloomy & grimy seems as if a suicide hung from every rafter within.—No open space—no squares or parks. You suffocate for room.—You pass close together. The cafes of the Turks. Dingy holes, faded splendor, moth eaten, on both sides wide seats or divans where the old musty Turks sit smoking like conjurors.—Saw in certain kiosks (pavilions) the crowns of the late Sultans. You look through gilt gratings & between many[1] curtains of lace, at the sparkling things. Near the mosque of Sultan Solyman saw the cemetery of his family—big as that of a small village, all his wives & children & servants. All gilt & carved. The women's tombs carved without heads (women no souls). The Sultan Solyman's tomb & that of his three brothers in a kiosk. Gilded like mantle ornaments.

Sunday Dec. 14. Three Sabbaths[2] a week in Constantinople. Friday, Turks; Sat, Jews; Sunday, Romanists, Greeks & Armenians.—At 8. A M crossed over the 2d bridge to Stamboul to ride round the Walls. Passed between wall & Golden Horn through Greek & Jew quarters, and came

[1]Other possible readings are "heavy" or "wavy."
[2]*Sundays* was written first, but crossed out.

outside the land wall in view of Sweet Waters, which run inland & end in beautiful glades. Rode along the land wall. By this wall Constantinople was taken by the Turks & the last of the Constantines fell in their defence. Four miles of massiveness, with huge square towers—a Tower of London—every 150 yards or so. In many parts rent by earthquakes. The towers especially. Great cracks & fissures. In one tower you see a jaw of light opening; the riven parts stand toppling like inverted pyramids. Evergreen vines mantling them. 4 walls parallel—added defences. The strength of the masonry shows, that when by earthquake the summit of a tower has been thrown down, it has slid off retaining its integrity—not separating, but rubbing like a rockslide. In the wide tracks, they cultivate them—garden spots—very rich & loamy—here fell the soldiers of Constantine—sowed in corruption & raised in potatoes.[1]—These walls skirted by forrests of cemetery—the cypresses growing thick as firs in a Scotch plantation. Very old—a primeval look—weird. The walls seem the inexorable bar between the mansions of the living & the dungeons of the dead.—Outside the wall here

[1]Melville seems to have cherished this as an apt and witty observation; in the course of the journal he repeats it three or four times.

is a Greek Church (for name see G.B.) Very beautiful, new upon an ancient site. (The miraculous fish here)[1] Decorated with banners of the virgin &c. A beautiful cave chapel—a fountain of holy water—Greeks come here & wash & burn a candle. All round under the trees people smoking nargiles, drinking & eating, & riding. Gay crowds. Greek Sunday. Rode to the wall-end at Sea of Marmora. The water dashes up against the foundations here for 6 miles to the Seraglio. Went in to the Seven Towers. 200 feet high, 2 overthrown. Immense thickness. Top of walls a soil & sod. Like walking on a terrace. Seven-sided enclosure. bases at angles. Superb view of the city & sea. Dungeons —inscriptions.—Soldiers—A mosque. Immensely long ride back within the walls. Lonely streets.

[1]The Church of the Fountain of Life, commonly known as the Shrine of Our Lady of the Fishes, destroyed in 1821 by the Janissaries, and rebuilt in 1849. The legend is, that a monk who was told that the Turks had taken the town exclaimed: "It is just as likely that these fish I am frying should jump out of this pan into their native element, as it is that the Infidels should ever be able to take this city." When lo! the fish at once returned to life, jumped out of the pan, and landed in a basin of water in the courtyard. The last and only descendants of these miraculous fish transmit to the water in which they drag out their miserable days, virtue to cure all diseases. See *A Guide to Constantinople* by Demetrius Coufopoulos, London, 1906, pp. 82-83.

Passed under an arch of the acqueduct of Valens (?)[1] In these lofty arches, ivied & weather-beaten, & still grand, the ghost of Rome seems to stride with disdain of the hovels of this part of Stamboul.—Overtopping houses & trees &c.—Recrossed the 2d bridge to Pera. Too late for the Dancing Dervishes. Saw their convent. Reminded me of the Shakers.—Went towards the cemeteries of Pera. Great resort on summer evenings. Bank of the Bosphorus—like Brooklyn heights. From one point a superb view of Sea of Marmora & Princes Isles & Scutari.—Armenian funerals winding through the streets. Coffin covered with flowers borne on a bier. Wax candles burn on each side in daylight. Boys & men chanting alternately. Striking effect, winding through the narrow lanes.—Saw a burial. Armenian. Juggling & incantations of the priests—making signs &c.—Nearby, saw a woman over a new grave—no grass on it yet. Such abandonment of misery! Called to the dead, put her head down as close to it as possible; as if calling down a hatchway a cellar; besought—"Why dont you speak to me? My God!—It is I! Ah,—speak—but one word!"—All deaf.—So much for consolation.—This woman & her cries haunt me horribly.——

[1]Though Melville questioned it, he was correct.

Street sights.—The beauty of the human countenance. Among the women ugly faces a rare.—Singular these races so exceed ours in this respect. Out of every other window look faces (Jew, Greek, Armenian) which in England or America would be a cynosure in a ball room.—Wretched looking houses & filthy streets. Tokens of pauperism without the paupers.[1] Out of old shanties peep lovely girls. like lillies & roses growing in cracked flower-pots. Very shy & coy looking. Many houses walled. Lower story no windows. Great gates like fortresses. Sign of barbarism. Robbers. Lattices to Turkish houses—little windows. Confusion of the streets—no leading one. No clue. Hopelessly lost.—Immense loads carried by porters.—Camels, donkeys, mules, horses. &c.—These Constantinople bridges exceed London bridges for picturesqueness. Contrast between London Bridge & these. Kayacks darting under the wooden arches. Spread about like swarm of ants, when their hill is invaded. On either side rows of Turkish craft of uniform build & height, stand like troops presenting arms. Masts of black English steamers. Guide boys on the bridge. Greeks. beautiful faces, lively, loquacious. Never wearied leaning over the balustrade & talking with them.—Viewed from bridge, the great mosques are shown to be

[1]In the right margin, boxed, is written: *For Note.*

built[1] most judiciously on the domed hills of the city. Fine effect. Seems a spreading, still further, of the tent. *Monday Dec 15.* Utterly used up last night. This morning felt as if broken on the wheel.—At eleven oclock went out without guide. Mounted the Genoese Tower. A prodigious structure. 60 feet in diameter. 200 or more high. Walls 12 feet thick. Stair in wall instead of at the tower's axis. Peculiar plan of the stairs. "Backshesh." Terminates in a funnel-shaped affair, like a minaret. The highest loft nest of pigeons. From the gallery without, all round, another glorious view. (Three great views of Constantinople) All important to one desirous to learn something of the bearings of Pera &c. After much study succeeded in understanding the way to the two great bridges. Came down, & crossed the first bridge. There took a boy-guide to the bazar. (All the way from the G. Tower down steep hill to bridge, a steady stream of people) Immense crowds on the Constantinople side. Way led up steps into large court surrounding mosque. (Mosque bazarr.)[2] Then clothes bazar, most busy scenes; all the way to the bazar by this route—crowds, crowds, crowds—From the Fez caps, the way seemed paved with tiles.[3]—The Bazarr is formed

[1]Melville wrote "build."
[2]In pencil, above the line.
[3]In pencil, above the line, is written: *fields of clover.*

of innumerable[1] narrow aisles, overarched; and along the sides looks like rows of show-cases, a sort of sofa-counter before them (where lady customers recline) and a man in each. Persian bazarr, superb. Pawnbrokers here, money changers, fellows with a bushel or two of coins of all nations, handling their change like pedlers of nuts.[2]—Rug merchants, (Angora wool) £10 for small one.—After dismissing my boy, was followed for two or three hours by an infernal Greek, & confederates. Dogged me; in & out & through the Bazaar. I could neither intimidate or elude them. Began to feel nervous; remembered that much of the fearful interest of Schiller's Ghost—Seer[3] hangs upon being followed in Venice by an Armenian. The mere mysterious, persistent, silent following. At last escaped them. Went to the Aga Janissary's. Tower of Fire Watchmen. An immense column of the Saracenic order. Colossal Saracenic. Saw drill of Turk troops here. Disciplining the barbarians.[4]—Looked at the burnt Column again. Base bedded in humus. It leans, is split & chipped

[1]Reading debatable.

[2]In the right margin, in pencil: (Cairo).

[3]In *Early Dramas and Romances* of Frederick Schiller (Bohn's Standard Library, 1853) 375 ff. This was the only available translation when Melville wrote this.

[4]Though this reading is questionable, I believe it is correct, and that Melville is speaking ironically, as when in

& cracked. Of a smoky purple color. Is garlanded round with laurel (chisseled) at distances. (Croton water pipes on end)—Street scenes. Gilded carriages of style of Hogarths carriages. Yellow boots daintily worn by the ladies in the mud.—Intricacy of the place. No way to get along the water-side—but by labyrinths of back lanes.—Strange books in the Mosque bazaar.—Englishman at dinner. Invited me to Buyukdereh—Gave me a shake down &c. Said nothing would tempt him to go by night through Galata. Assassinations every night.—His cottage on Bosphorus attacked by robbers. &c. (The Bosphorus)

Tuesday Dec 16th At 8½ A. M took steamer up the Bosphorus to Buyukdereh. — Magnificent! The whole scene one pomp of art & nature. Europe & Asia here show their best. A challenge of continents, whereby the successively alternate sweeps of the shores both sides seem to retire from every new proffer of beauty, again in some grand prudery to advance with a bolder bid, and thereupon again

Clarel (Vol. 2, p. 205), in an arraignment of the worldliness of Christendom, he says:

"But preach and work:
You'll civilize the barbarous Turk—
Nay, all the East may reconcile:
That done, let Mammon take the wings of even
And mount and civilize the saints in heaven."

& again retiring, neither willing to retreat from the contest of beauty.—Myrtle, Cypress, Cedar—evergreens.—Catch glimpse of Euxine from Buyukdereh. The water clear as Ontario—the banks natural quays, shelving off like those of a canal. Large vessels go close along shore.—The palaces of the Sultan—the pleasure-houses—palaces of ambassadors—The white foam breaks on these white steps as on long lines of coral reefs. One peculiarity is the introduction of ocean into inland recesses. Ships anchor at the foot of ravines, deep among green basins, where the only canvas you would look for would be tents.—A gallery of ports & harbors, formed by the interexchange of promontory & bay. Many parts like the Highlands of the Hudson, magnified. Porpoises sport in the blue; & large flights of pigeons overhead go through evolutions like those of armies. The sun shining on the palaces. View from the heights of Buyukdereh. "Royal Albert" Euxine in sight from Buyukdereh. A chain of Lake Georges. No wonder the Czars have always coveted the capital of the Sultans. No wonder the Russian among his firs sighs for these myrtles. —Cedar & Cypress the only trees about the capital. —The Cypress a green minaret, & blends with the stone ones. Minaret perhaps[1] derived from cypress

[1]Debatable reading.

shape. The intermingling of the dark tree with the bright spire expressive of the intermingling of life & death.—Holyday aspect of the Bosphorus—The daisies are tipped with a crimson dawn, the very soil from which they spring has a ruddy hue.—Kiosks & fountains. One is amazed to see[1] such delicate & fairy-like structures out of doors. One would think the elements would visit them too rudely; that they would melt away like—castles of confectionery. Profuse sculpture & gilding & painting.—The bays sweep round in great ampitheaters.—Coming back from Bosphorus, stood on the First Bridge. Curious to stand amid these millions of fellow beings, some of whom seem not unwilling to accept our civilization, but with one consent rejecting much of our morality & all of our religion. (*Note*) Aspect of the Bridge like that of a Grand Fancy Ball. (An immense Persian Rug.) 1500000 men the actors. Banvard[2] should paint a

[1]Debatable reading.

[2]I have by me, published by John Putnam, Boston, 1847, a work entitled: *Description of Banvard's Panorama of the Mississippi River, Painted on THREE MILES OF CANVAS: exhibiting a view of country 1200 miles in length, extending from the Mouth of the Missouri River to the City of New Orleans; being by far The Largest Picture ever executed by Man.* John Banvard (1815-1891) also wrote nearly two thousand poems, two plays that got produced, and published a variety of volumes (one to teach a system of shorthand of his own invention).

few hundred miles of this pageant of moving procession. Pedlars of all sorts & hawkers. Confectionery carried on head. A chain of malefactors with iron rings about their necks—Indian file. Porters immense bundles, brains doing the office of sinews. Others carrying bundles with poles, hands resting on each others shoulders. Military officers followed by running footmen. Ladies in yellow slippers. "Arabas." Horses, whose docility & gentleness is such as horseriders as any other foot passengers.[1]—Taking toll on the bridge (Three or four men). Splendid barges of the Pashas darting under the arches. (Ant-hill of caiques)[2] A gentleman followed by his Greek servants on horseback. An officer conversing with his confidential[3]. A Black eunuch followed by white servants in great state. Servant. [Negro Musselmen &c (caparisons)][4] Sherbert sellers on bridge-side. An Arab . . . .[5]. Or a Georgian. with tall cap. The soldiers. The droves

In 1851 an anonymous biography was published of him. For other panoramas of Banvard, and for the vogue of panoramas at this time, see Professor George C. D. Odell's *Annals of the New York Stage*, N. Y., 1931, Vol. V., p. 402 and Vol. VII, pp. 192, 525, 536, 541.

[1]This is a hopeless sentence.

[2]In the left margin, in ink.

[3]A very dubious reading.

[4]Above the line, in pencil.

[5]Illegible.

of sheep—shepherds marching in sheep clothing in advance. A file of loaded horses—sacks of flour. A drove of donkeys—everybody giving them a poke.—You hear names of Yusef, Hassan, Hamet (Arabian Nights) bandied on all sides. A Mosque at end of bridge. The Bazarr Mosque. Shaving heads in its court &c. Road to Bazarr leads through this court. Visited Mosque of Achmed (6 towers) Forecourt like a huge conservatory. 20 small cupolas & domes. A double gallery. A verandah without, and a collonade within. A fountain in the middle. Columns of variously colored marbles & mosaic. Heaps of old traps, old capotes being cut up by beggars. bales with marks. Pile of old hoops rusting. Pile of old haversacks and belts & spoons & kettles. Grated windows look between the double galleries. Beautiful effect. Outside, under gallery, ruins of penstocks, with stone footstool below, for worshippers to wash feet &c. Within, four vast pillars supports to the dome, like towers (white marble) Most perfect specimen of the mosque. Regular square, inside. Small domes & half domes. —In the "towers" are fountains. Birds perched among the chandeliers, flying about

[1]Continued in leather covered book
"bought in Constantinople"—Dec 16—1856—

[1]In pencil, in a large clear hand.

"Bobby luck".—Dispute whether any men are content. Foolish fellow found. Said he was content —perfectly. Sure?—Yes.—Never annoyed by anything? No.—Think.—No—But think—Oh Yes, there is one thing, when I go into the streets all the boys cry out There goes Silly Bobby.

Captains wives at sea. Ship cast away while Captain holding his wife's head—sea-sick.

The juggler's exposure in Edinburgh &c.

(Story of the Pantaloons in the Indes)

(Taylor's offer to be cicerone.)

(This is the end of the first of the two journals)

Bought this book at Bazaar in Constantinople.
Herman Melville's Journal.

[1]A pocket-compass were very useful in Constantinople.
[[2]Pera, the headquarters of ambassadors, and where also an unreformed diplomacy is carried on by swindlers, gamblers, cheats, no place in the world fuller of knaves.
[Contrast of Dardenelles with Sts: of Gibraltar.
[Salonica is, next to Constantinople, the chief place of commerce in European Turkey.
[Entering Europe by back door
[Man is a noble animal, splendid in epitaphs &c—
(Inscription of the onions in Cheops)[3]
[Lore of the "Bible"—Amsterdam—like the "Press"]
The Burnt Districts.

Constantinople

Tuesday, *Dec 16* [Continued from Small Journal]
1856[4]

[1]In pencil.

[2]In the left margin, in pencil: *For the Story*. I cannot discover that this projected story survives.

[3]See Herodotus, Book 2, Chapter 125.

[4]In pencil.

Wandered about in vicinity of Hippodrome till nearly dusk; lost myself, & finally came out at a gate on the Sea of Marmora. Returned to Tophanna by kayeck. Interesting appearance of the walls here. Owing to the heigth of the shore above the sea, the fortifications here present a wall on the water side, but only a parapet on the land. Hence, from the sea, the houses look immensely lofty; they are of all shapes; in some parts their windows are formed by the open spaces of the battlements. In some parts, there are balconies. Several gates & archways are to be seen walled up. Collonades are disclosed, closed up. Pilasters. The fall, or rather crumbling away of the wall at one angle discloses a solitary column of white marble, looking strange as the resurrection of a body masoned up in a tomb. Reminded me of the Abbotsford walls—only, on a grand scale. Where huge masses of the masonry have fallen, they look like rocks, in confused heaps, the mortar as hard as the tile & stone.—At dinner today the French attache estimated the population of Constantinople, suburbs, & banks of Bosphorus at 1,500,000. A moderate estimate, judging from the swarms.—The fortress of Mamud II on Bosphorus built in the likeness of the Arabic letters of his name. Conveys an idea of his spirit. Plenty who with a flourish skate their names on ice, but few

who solidly build them up in walls upon the enduring rocks.—Extraordinary aspect of this fortress from the sea.
Wednesday Dec 17 Spent the day revisiting the Seraglio &c.—Owing to its peculiar form St: Sophia viewed near to, looks as partly underground; as if you saw but the superstructure of some immense temple, yet to be disinterred. You step *down* to enter. The dome has a kind of dented appearance, like crown of old hat. Must inevitably cave in one of these days. Within dome has appearance (from its flatness) of an immense sounding board. A firmament of masonry. [It rests on 4 arches, two of which are blind. (Massy buttresses.) The other open. Seems to rest here on cobweb. (Entrance in them, like caves).][1] The interior a positive appropriation of space. The precious marbles, of the interior. the worshipping—head prostration.—In the part of the town near Old Seraglio—silent appearance of the streets. Strange houses. Rows of quaint old sideboards, cupboards, beauforts, tall Nuremburg clocks. Lanes & allies of them. Seraglio. (Silence of Seraglio as house of prayer[1]) Many prohibited spots. The Seraglio (proper) seems to be a quadrangle, on the hill, where buildings present blank walls, buttressed, outside; but within open.

[1]Along the left margin.

Cypress overpeer the walls in some parts. Grand view from Seraglio Point—Marmora, Bosphorus, Scutari.—The courts & grounds of Seraglio have a strange, enchanted sort of look.—*The dogs*, roam about in bands like prairie wolves. No masters. No Turk seems to have a dog. None domesticated. Nomadic. Against religion to kill them. Scavangers of the city. Terrible outcries at times. At night. Fighting of the dogs. Strange to come upon pack of them in some lonely lane. Mostly yellow, with long sharp noses. Some much scarred, others mangy. See them lying amidst refuse, hardly tell them from it. —same color. See them over a dead horse on the beach.—Wandering about came across Black Hole in the street. Did not enter far.—Harem (sacred) on board steam boats. Lattic division. Ladies pale, slight noses, regular features, fine busts. Look like nuns in their plain dress, but with a roundness of bust not belonging to that character. Perfect decorum between sexes. No ogling. No pertness. No looking for admiration. No Cyprians. No drunkards. Saw not a single one, though liquor is sold.—Industry.—Beauty of fountain near St: Sophia. Gilding—Grapes & foliage.

Thursday Dec 18 In morning took caique, & crossed the Bosphorus to Scutari. Luxurious sailing. Cushioned like ottoman. You lie in the boat's bottom. Body beneath the surface. A boat bed. Kaik a sort of carved trencher or tray.—Fleet of fishermen, at mouth of Golden Horn. Calm of water. Tide-rips. Sun shining on Sultan's palaces. Sunrise opposite the Seraglio. *As Constantinople is finest site for capital, so Seraglio for pleasure-grounds, in the world.*[1] —Great barracks at Scutari: Noble view of Constantinople & up Bosphorus. Cemeteries like Black Forrest. Thuringian look. Roads passing through it. Beautiful daisies. The quays. The water mosque. The hills & beach.—*General Thoughts about Constantinople.* As for its mud, mere wet pollen of a flower.—Tenedos wine on table—The Negro Musselman. Unlike other dispersed nations (Jews, Armenians, Gypsies) who proof against proselytism adhere to the faith first delivered to their fathers. Negro as indifferent to forms as horse to caparisons. (*Turks want to be buried in Asia.*)[2] At 4 P. M. sailed in steamer Acadia for Alexandria, via Smyrna. It was sunset ere we rounded Seraglio Point. Glorious night. Scutari & its heights, glowed like sapphire. Wonderful clearness of air. As a promontory is covered with trees, terraced up clear to its top, so Constantinople with houses. Long line of walls.—Out into Sea of Marmora.

[1]Opposite this sentence, in the left margin: *For Note.*
[2]Along the left margin.

Friday Dec 19 Passed through Dardenelles at day-break. Showers of rain. Cleared off. Passed Plain of Troy, Mount Ida beyond. Passed the tumulus of Achilles &c. Steered in between Tenedos & the main. Passed a town & harbor of Tenedos; a promontory in the midst of the harbor covered with massive fortifications,—the work of the old Genoese. Passed Cape Baba crowned with a fort protecting a town on high land. The Asiatic coast all along lofty with ranges of mountains in the background—a yellow look. Steered in between Mytelene & the main. A large & lovely island, covered with olive trees. They make much wine. The whole island green from beach to hill-top.—a dark rich bronzy green, in marked contrast with the yellow & parched aspect of most other isles of the Archipelego.—Asia looks in color like those Asiatic lions one sees in menageries—lazy & torpid.—Many beautiful hamlets seen on Mytelene. It has one fine landlocked harbor in the middle of the isle.—Near sunset came to anchor for the night in a little bay of Mytelene, so as to have the benefit of daylight for getting into Smyrna, a ticklish harbor. Sent a boat off to get soundings. A boat came from shore; brought olives & figs. According to a chart of "Mouth of Dardenelles & Plain of Troy" in the Captain's possession, I see that the whole coast hereabouts & for some ways inland is covered with ruins of great antiquity. [Sailed through Besika Bay partly sheltered by Isle Tenedos, where the E & F fleets first joined in 1853.]

Saturday Dec 20. At two in the morning up anchor at Mytelene, and by daylight were entering the bay of Smyrna. A very spacious one, thirty miles deep & 7 or 8 wide, with villages nestling in the hillsides, and lofty mountains all round. The town is at the end of the bay, and where for a little it stretches along a declivity, it looks, from the lowness of the houses, their flat roofs red-tiled like a feild of broken pottery. On Mount Pagus behind the town is an old castle, conspicuous from the sea.—Met the steamer Egyptian in port; saw Cap. Tate. A steamer grounded & one towing her off. Went ashore & called up American Consul, a Greek. Spent an hour conversing with him & his brother. Got a guide (a grave ceremonious man with a frogged coat carrying a silver mounted sword in a velvet scabbard in one hand, and a heavy silver mounted cowhide in the other) and went to Bazarr, to see the slaves. Failed. Went up Mt Pagus. A large circuit. The interior strewn over with fragments of stones, looking like a barren moor. Commands a superb view of bay & town of Smyrna.

An old ruinous mosque within. A Boston name written there. Descended, & went to the Caravan Bridge, a great resort on holy days, and country gate of the town. Here passed a constant succession of trains of camels, horses, mules, & donkeys. Sometimes a horse leading a camel-train, sometimes a donkey, sometimes a donkey also following. Horsemen with arms. Buffalo.—The camel a most ungainly creature From his long curved and crane-like neck, (which he carries stiffly like a clergyman in a stiff cravat) his feathery-looking forelegs, & his long lank hind ones, he seems a cross between an ostrich & a gigantic grasshopper. His hoof is spongy, & covered with hair to the ground, so that walking through these muddy lanes, he seems stilting along on four mops.—[Carries his neck out like a tortoise. Tail like long eel, driver holds it & steers him. Has a way of turning his head so that his face & tail face you together.][1] [A sort of saw-buck.—swaying of the rider—height. Motion increases as in mast of ship. Camel seems built by nature with special precaution against man's use. The hump in way of saddle, but man outwits Nature here.][2] [Camel dung like pancakes stuck against houses, to dry. Loads of them on men's heads.

[1]Along the left margin.
[2]Along the right margin.

Coals.][1]—The cemeteries very interesting, broken columns & capitals of great antiquity strewn among the broken tomb-stones; sometimes a dilapidated tomb-stone is seen composed of an old column—a double ruin. Cypresses very high & pillar-like.

Sunday Dec 21 Called with Captain Tate upon his agent, living in a handsome house upon the Marinar. Married to a Greek lady, with a child that speaks as yet only Greek, her father a Scotchman. With reference to the American Mission here the Agent said it was about discontinued; a hopeless affair; all the converts made, mercenary ones. Attended chapel at the English Consulate. Very flat affair; the chaplain, however, a curiosity.—There dined today on board "Arcadia" C. Orpheus, C Tate, C. Eustace & self. Much talk of India voyages.

Monday Dec 22 Went ashore in the morning, interested in the curious appearance of strings of loaded camels passing through the narrow & crowded covered ways of the Bazaar. Heard a good deal about the commerce of England with Turkey. The Turkish manufactures almost at an end. The people of Manchester imitate exactly every fabric in the world. Cotton & silk imported from Turkey & returned in the form of Turkish manufactures, being retailed in the Bazaars as such, & as such articles

[1]Along the right margin.

are sometimes taken home as curiosities to England & America by travelers. Copper is found in Turkey & quantities are sent to England to be made into coin for the Sultan. The English manufacturers alloy it, & return a base metal for the pure, charging for the process. In the "Egyptian" there were several casks of unstamped copper coin, for Constantinople.—Altho' it was a little rainy the morning of our arrival here, yet ever since, the weather has been very beautiful, like fine Spring days at home.—This evening an odd affair between C.Orpheus & his first officer, to which I was an unavoidable listener.

Tuesday Dec 23d Expect to sail today for Syra, so did not go ashore. Two passengers came off today, one a Greek officer, a comical looking fellow.—Got under weigh for Syra about 3 P. M. Fine sail down the bay. Came on blowing a gale outside, but by morning pleasant weather. Strong winds of short continuance here. Approached Syra by Myconi Passage between the islands of Myconi & Tinos. Many other isles scattered about. Among others, Delos, of a most barren aspect, however flowery in fable. I heard it was peculiarly sterile. Patmos, too, not remote; another disenchanting isle. Tinos is a large island, with numerous small hamlets (60 of them I was told) no trees, but they cultivate the grape. Each little village has its little church. They are Catholics or Turks. Wholly agricultural people. Said to be 365 isles in the Archipelegoe, one for every day in the year. Entering Syra harbor, I was again struck by the appearance of the town on the hill. The houses seemed clinging round its top, as if desperate for security, like shipwrecked men about a rock beaten by billows. A Greek on board tells me that, escaped from the massacres of Scio & Mytelene, certain Greeks escaped here in 1821, & founded the town. Syra is the most considerable place in the Archipelego, &, for commerce, perhaps in all Greece. Came to anchor at 12. M. Put us in quarantine for 24 hours (to begin from time of leaving Smyrna) tho' no case of illness on board. C. storms at the nuisance.

Wednesday, Dec 24th Included in preceding day.

Thursday Dec 25 CHRISTMAS.[1] Today appears to be no holyday among the Greeks. Or theirs is the old style of almanack; people are so busy here I cannot learn which.—Went ashore to renew my impressions of the previous visit. The Greek, of any class, seems a natural dandy. His dress, though a laborer, is that of a gentleman of leisure. This flowing, & graceful costume, with so much of pure ornament about it & so little fitted for labor, must needs have

[1]In 1849, Christmas, Melville was away from home: at Portsmouth, awaiting the ship to take him back to America.

been devised in some Golden Age. But surviving in the present, is most picturesquely out of keeping with the utilities.—Some of the poorest sort present curious examples of what may be called the decayed picturesque.[1] The Greeks have a great partiality for the tassel. This seems emblematic. You see one going about the quay displaying in every tempting mode, a long graceful tassel,—holding it up admiringly.—On the Custom House quay lie bales of tobacco, jars of oil, and what you would call rows of dead goats, but which prove to be goat skins, filled, not with the flesh of goats, but the blood of the grape.—In the cafes, much card playing, all through the day. Syra is the depot for the Archipelego. They export, sponges, raisins, tobacco, fruit, olive oil &c. Their imports are hardware, & cloths, all from England. They have quite a ship-yard here. Two Greek men-of-war lie here; little fellows, yawls-of-war one might call them.—One motive for building the old town on the hill

[1]*Picturesque* was a term that particularly interested Melville, and in *At The Hostelry* (*Poems* pp. 359-377) "the Marquis evokes—and from the Shades, as would seem—an inconclusive debate as to the exact import of a current term significant of that one of the manifold aspects of life and nature which under various forms all artists strive to submit to canvas. A term, be it added, whereof the lexicons give definitions more lexicographical than satisfactory." It is an endless discussion of the "picturesque" which gets nowhere.

was fear of pirates, & as a defence from them as well as the Turks. After things became more favorable, they descended, & built the new town along the water.—In the afternoon some Greek ladies came off, passengers for Alexandria. At five P. M. got under weigh—Farewell to Syra and the Greeks & away for Egypt & the Arabs.

Friday Dec 26. Last night the Captain mildly celebrated the day with a glass of Champagne.—Contrast between the Greek isles & those of the Polynesian archipelego.[1] The former have lost their virginity. The latter are fresh as at their first creation. The former look worn, and are meagre, like life after enthusiasm is gone. The aspect of all of them is sterile & dry. Even Delos whose flowers rose by miracle in the sea, is now a barren moor, & to look upon the bleak yellow of Patmos, who would ever think that a God had been there.—No shoals in the Archipelego; you may sail close to any of the isles, which makes easy navigation.—(Many of islands composed of pure white marble. Islanders retain expression of ancient statues.)[2] This morning was invited by Chief Engineer to inspect his department. The furnaces were a fearful

[1] In *Timoleon* (*Poems*, p. 288) in verses entitled *The Archipelago* Melville elaborates this contrast.

[2] Along the left margin.

scene. A hell in the hull. All day a head wind & bad sea. Passengers mostly laid up. The Greeks invisible. Passed pretty close to Scarpanti,—rugged & barren—Rhodes in sight.

Saturday Dec 27. Sea gone down with the wind. Towards noon fine weather, transparent air & a Syrian sun, rather scorching to the cheek. Expect to reach Alexandria tomorrow early. Saw in "Sailing Directions" brief account of Jaffa. oldest seaport in the world (some say it was a port before Noah) Rocks & sands, barren & dreary look.—

Sunday Dec 28 At early morning came in sight of Alexandria Light-house, and shortly after, saw Pompey's Pillar. Landed at 10. A. M. Donkey to hotel, near which garden of the date palm. Pompey's pillar looks like huge stick of candy after having been long sucked. Cleopatra's Needles—one of them down & covered over. Rode along banks of Canal of Mohammed and to Garden of the Pasha.

Monday Dec. 29th Called at Consul's for my passport. Mr. De Leon formerly political literary man at Washington. Met officers of the U.S.F. Constellation. Went to the Catacombs on the sea.

Tuesday Dec 30. To Cairo, arrived there at 4 P. M. put up at Shepherd's. Walked about the square with Dr Lockwood.

Wednesday Dec 31. To the Pyramids; through the

town to the Citadel & back to Shepherd's at nightfall.—Never shall forget this day. It racks me that I can only spend one day in Cairo, owing to steamer.

THURSDAY JAN 1st, 1857. From Cairo to Alexandria. Put up at Victoria Hotel.

Friday Jan 2d. Expected to have sailed today for Jaffa. But steamer not arrived. Spent day reading a book on Palestine.

Saturday Jan 3d. Steamer for Jaffa will not sail till tomorrow, so that I am wearied to death with two days in Alexandria which might have been delightfully spent in Cairo. But travellers must expect these things.—I will now without any order jot down my impressions of Cairo, ere they grow dim. —It seems one booth and Bartholemew Fair—a grand masquerade of mortality.—Several of the thoroughfare covered at vast heigth with old planks & matting, so that the street has the light of a closed verandah. In one case this matting extends from mosque to mosque, where they are opposite. The houses seem a collection of old orchestras, organs, proscenium boxes,—or like masses of old furniture (grotesque) lumbering a garret & covered with dust. Lattice-work of the projecting windows. With little square holes, just large enough to contain the head. Curious aspect of women's faces peeping out. Most of the houses built of stone of a brownish white. Some of the streets of private houses are like tunnels from meeting overhead of projecting windows &c. Like night at noon. Sometimes high blank walls—mysterious passages,— dim peeps at courts & wells in shadow. [Streets leading through arch of abandoned mosque. The gates dividing one part of town from another. Jew Quarters.][1] Great numbers of uninhabited houses in the lonelier parts of the city. Their dusty, cadaverous ogerish look. Ghostly, & suggestive of all that is weird. Haunted houses & Cock Lanes. Ruined mosques, domes knocked in like stoven boats. Others, upper part empty & desolate with broken rafters & dismantled windows; (rubbish) below, the dirty rites of religion. Aspect of the thoroughfares like London streets on Saturday night. All the world gossiping & marketing,—but in picturesque costumes. Crookedness of the streets—multitudes of blind men—worst city in the world for them. Flies on the eyes at noon. Nature feeding on man. Contiguity of desert & verdure, splendor & squalor, gloom & gayety; numerous blind men going about led, Children opthalmic. Too much light & no defence against it.—The antiquity of Egypt stamped upon individuals.—Appearance of the women. Thing for the face. Black crape hanging like trunk

[1]Along the left margin.

of elephant. Profusion of jewelry. Brass on face. Staining the eyes (black) & fingernails. (yellow)—Some in fine silks & on donkeys. [Streets great place for studying the beard.][1] Animated appearance of the population. Turks in carriages, with Osmanli drivers & footmen; sitting back proudly & gazing round on the people still with the air of conquerors. Footmen running ahead with silver tipped bamboos. Rapid driving, shouts of the driver. Camels carrying water in panniers of leather. Carrying straw in bags—Donkey loads of green grass.—of stones—of pottery—of garden stuff—of chickens in wicker panniers—of babies in panniers—Long strings of them. Turk on donkey, resting his pipe vertically before him on pommel. Grave & tranquil.

View from Citadel. Built by Saladin. Cairo nipped between two deserts—the one leading to Suez & the Red Sea, the other the Lybian Desert.—Dust colored city. The dust of ages. The Nile—the green —desert—pyramids. Minarets unlike those of Constantinople which gleam like lighthouses,—but of an ashy color, and wonderfully venerable. Citadel perched on solid rock. Within, wall of decayed fortresses. You stand at base of forecourt of Mosque to get the view, looking sheer down some 200 feet

[1]Along the left margin.

on tops of deserted houses, to immense square full of people, and near the spot where the Memlook saved himself by leaping his house.[1] Mosque (new) splendid court & colonnade. Within, green & gold. Square, with four half-domes. Superb pillars. Alabaster. Could make brooches of them. Mosque of Hassan on the square below citadel. Finest in Cairo.

PYRAMIDS. Scamper to them with officers on donkeys. Rapid passing of crowds upon the road; following of the donkey-boys &c. [In heyday holyday spirits arrived at the eternal sorrows of the pyramids. Cross Nile in boats.[2] In[3] Roda, pavilions & kiosks & gardens. Donkeys crossing, rapid current, muddy banks. Pyramids from distance purple like mountains. Seem high & pointed, but flatten & depress as you approach. Vapors below summits.

[1]See *Clarel* (Vol. 1, p. 89):

"Like Emim Bey the Mameluke.
He—armed, and happily, mounted well—
Leaped the inhuman citidel
In Cairo; fled—yea, bleeding, broke
Through shouting lanes his breathless way
Into the desert;"—&c.—

And *Clarel* (Vol. 2, p. 71) for a lyric which begins:

"The Bey, The Emir, and Mameluke lords
Charged down on the field in a grove of swords:"

[2]The reading may be "boots."

[3]The reading may be "Ise."

Kites sweeping & soaring around, hovering right over apex. at angles, like broken cliffs. Table-rock overhanging, adhering solely by mortar. Sidelong look when midway up. Pyramids on a great ridge of sand. You leave the angle, and ascend hillock of sand & ashes & broken mortar & pottery to a point, & then go along a ledge to a path &c. zig-zag routes. As many routes as to cross the Alps—The Simplon, Great St: Bernard &c. Mules on Andes. Caves—platforms. Looks larger midway than from top or bottom. Precipice on precipice, cliff on cliff. Nothing in Nature gives such an idea of vastness. A balloon to ascend them. View of persons ascending, Arab guides in flowing white mantles. Conducted as by angels up to heaven. Guides so tender. Resting. Pain in the chest. Exhaustion. Must hurry. None but the phlegmatic go deliberately. Old man with the spirits of youth—long looked for this chance—tried the ascent, half way—failed—brought down. Tried to go into the interior—fainted—brought out—leaned against the pyramid by the entrance—pale as death. Nothing so pathetic. Too much for him; oppressed by the massiveness & mystery of the pyramids. I myself too. A feeling of awe & terror came over me. Dread of the Arabs. Offering to lead me into a side-hole. The Dust. Long arched way,—then down as in a coal shaft. Then as in mines, under the sea. [At one moment seeming in the Mammoth Cave. Subterranean gorges, &c.][1] The stooping & doubling. I shudder at idea of ancient Egyptians. It was in these pyramids that was conceived the idea of Jehovah. Terrible mixture of the cunning and awful. Moses learned in all the lore of the Egyptians. The idea of Jehovah born here.—[When I was at top, thought it not so high—sat down on edge. Looked below—gradual nervousness & final giddiness & terror. [Entrance of pyramids like shoot for coal or timber. Horrible place for assassination. As long as earth endures some vestige will remain of the pyramids. Nought but earthquake or geological revolution can obliterate them. Only people who made their mark, both in their masonry & their religion (through Moses). (These the steps Jacob lay at.)[1] [*Color of Pyramids same as desert.* Some of the stone (but few) friable; most of them hard as ever. The climate favors them. Pyramids not in line. Between, like Notch of White Mountains. *No vestige of moss upon them. Not the least. Other ruins ivied. Dry as tinder. No speck of green.* Arabs climb them like goats, or any other animal. Down one & up the other. Pyramids still loom before me—something vast, indefinite, incomprehensible, and

[1]Along the left margin.

awful.[1] Line of desert & verdure, plain as line between good & evil. An instant collision of alien elements. A long billow of desert forever hovers as in act of breaking, upon the verdure of Egypt. Grass near the pyramids, but will not touch them,—as if in fear or awe of them. Desert more fearful to look at than ocean. Theory of design of pyramids. Defense against desert. A line of them. Absurd. Might have been created with the creation.

The Sphynx. back to desert & face to verdure. Solid rock.—You ride through palms to the pyramids. You are carried across the mire &c by Arabs. The two black sheiks in black robes.—*The ride to the pyramids.* Passed succession of suburbs & villages—high walls with date palms below or heavy vines overhanging the walls. Across bridges, the party condensing & then expanding in disorderly dispersion. The acqueduct. The gates. Passed groves of palms, like temple of 1001 columns. [Beauty of the suburbs of Cairo. Long avenues of acacias; locusts &c. *Road to Shooha.* Processions of people.

Life at hotel. Magnitude of Shepherds, lofty ceilings, stone floors, iron beds, no carpets, thin mattresses, no feathers, blinds, moscho curtains.—All showing

[1]See *The Great Pyramid* and *In the Desert* (*Poems*, pp. 292-293)

the tropics. And that you are in the East is shown by fresh dates on table for desert, water in stone jars—(cool) waited on by Arabs—dragomen—clap your hands for servants.—Brilliant scene at late dinner—hard to believe you are near the pyramids. Yet some repose in fastidiousness.—

Appearance of the great square. Upon entering Cairo, saw the crescent & star—arms of Sultan in the sky. Large extent of square. Canal about it. Lower level than walks around. Avenues of acacias & other trees. Shrubs. Seems country. No fences. The booths & cafes. Leapers, tumblers, jugglers, smokers, dancers, horses, swings, (with bells) ṣherbert, &c. Lovely at evening. In morning, golden sun through foliage. Soft luxurious splendor of mornings. Dewy. Paradise melted & poured into the air. Soft intoxication; no wonder the people never drink wine. Wondered at the men in hotel drinking it —here.

Account of donkey & donkey boys. Wonderful endurance of both. Runs like deer (the boy). Stick in hand, barefooted & barelegged. Pounds the donkey, talks to him, remonstrates, advises. Donkey says nothing [☞ See Constantinople] Every one pushes him. Donkey is one of the best fellows in the world. It is the patience & honesty of the donkey that makes him so abused & despised. He is so useful & indispensable, that he is contemned. He is so unresisting. Tipe of honesty &c. As for his bray, that is the original Egyptian. Run about like rats. Their saddles very curious. High balled pommel. Thrown by donkey. A great love for them. Hacks.

[Climate of Egypt in winter is the reign of spring upon earth, & summer in the air, and tranquillity in the heat.

Ride to Cairo from Alexandria. The Delta. Like Mohawk Flats in Spring. Soil like moist pulverized manure. Seems spaded over. Barn-yard. 4 crops a year. Sugar, wheat, cotton.—Villages of unbaked brick. Wasps nests & mud pies. Beaver-dams. Pigeon houses, on dwellings, roofs covered with piles of husks & straw.—[No fences.] Cattle tethered in lines & eat clean on . . . .[1] Buffalo, camel, donkey. Palms. Villages like sand banks at distance. Approaching Cairo long avenues (raised above level) processions of people, crossing & recrossing at long distances. Encampment of troops. White soldiers. Cavalry in long strings.

[1]There are two words here that I can get no meaning out of; they look like *stight mach.*

Canal in ditch of R.R. irrigation. Dipping & machines. 3d class passengers. On top of cars. Noise & confusion of troops. Extra roof to cars. Turk squatting in baggage car on rug with his pipe. 2d class passengers. Turks & Egyptians. Jingle of scimiters & flash of silks. Smoking. Cross the Nile. Machine Canal boats, latteen (long) yard like well-sweep. Canal flowing between sand-hills. From the car (1st class) you seem in England. All else Egypt. Seems unreal & a panorama, beginning with Pompey's Pillar & ending with Cheops.[1]

Alexandria. Seems Mcadamed with the pulverized ruins of thousand cities. Every shovel full of earth dug over. The soil, deep loam, looks historical. The Grand Square. Lively aspect. Arabs looking in at windows. The sea is the principal point. Catacombs by it. R.R. extension driven right through. Acres. Wonderful appearance of the sea at noon. Sea & sky molten into each other. Pompey's Pillar like long stick of candy, well sucked. Cleopatra's needles close by hovels. One down & covered. Sighing of the waves. Cries of watchmen at night. Lanterns. Assassins. Sun strokes.

[1]See the note on John Banvard, pp. 35-36. As a matter of fact, Banvard did paint a panorama of the Nile, as well as one of Jerusalem and the Holy Land.

The Pyramids. The lines of stone do no seem like courses of masonry, but like strata of rocks. The long slope of crags & precipices. The vast plane. No wall, no roof. In other buildings, however vast, the eye is gradually innured to the sense of magnitude, by passing from part to part. But here there is no stay or stage. It is all or nothing. It is not the sense of height, (or breadth or length or depth that is stirred),[1] but the sense of immensity, that is stirred. After seeing the pyramid, all other architecture seems but pastry. Though I had but so short a time to view the pyramid, yet I doubt whether any time spent upon it, would tend to a more precise impression of it. As with the ocean, you learn as much of its vastness by the first five minutes glance as you would in a month, so with the pyramid. Its simplicity confounds you. Finding it vain to take in its vastness man has taken to sounding it & weighing its density; so with the pyramid, he measures the base, & computes the size of individual stones. It refuses to be studied or adequately comprehended. It still looms in my imagination, dim & indefinite. The tearing away of the casing, though it removed enough stone to build a walled-town, has not one whit subtracted from the apparent magnitude of the pyramid. It has had just the

[1]Added in pencil.

contrary effect. When the pyramid presented a smooth plane, it must have lost as much in impressiveness as the ocean does when unfurrowed. A dead calm of masonry. But now the ridges majestically diversify. It has been said in panegyric of some extraordinary works of man, that they affect the imagination like the works of Nature. But the pyramid affects one in neither way exactly. Man seems to have had as little to do with it as Nature. It was that supernatural creature, the priest. They must needs have been terrible (inventors)[1], those Egyptian wise men. And one seems to see that as out of the crude forms of the natural earth they could evoke by art the transcendent mass & symetry & . . . . . of the pyramid so out of the rude elements of the insignificant thoughts that are in all men, they could rear the transcendent conception of a God. But for no holy purpose was the pyramid founded. [Casts no shadow great part of day. Explorers . . . . .[2] out 30 miles in desert][3]

[1]Doubtful reading.
[2]Undecipherable.
[3]In pencil.

January 4th 1857. Sailed from Alexandria for Jaffa. 2d class passage. Many deck passengers Turks &c. *Jan 5th.* Fine day & warm. On deck all the time. *Jan 6th.* Early in the morning came in sight of Jaffa. A swell rolling, and saw the breakers before the town. Landed, not without some danger,—boatmen (Arabs) trying to play upon my supposed fears. Cunning dogs!—Employed a Jew dragoman to take me to Jerusalem.[1]—Crossed the plain of Sharon in sight of mountains of Ephraim. Arrived at Ramla & put up at alleged (hotel). At supper over broken crockery & cold meat, pestered by moschitos & fleas, dragoman said, "Dese Arab no know how to keep hotel" I fully assented. After horrible night, at 2 in the morning in saddle for Jerusalem.[2] The three shadows stalking on the plain by moonlight. Moon set, all dark. At day break found ourselves just entering the mountains. Pale olive of morning. Withered & desert country. Breakfast by ruined mosque—cave. Hot & wearisome ride over the arid hills.—Got to Jerusalem about 2 P. M.[3] Put up at Mediterranean Hotel. Kept by a German converted Jew, by name,

[1]About fifty-five miles distant.

[2]With forty miles still to go.

[3]This trip from Jaffa to Jerusalem is retraced in *Clarel* Vol. I, p. 4.

Hauser. Hotel[1] overlooks on one side Pool of Hezekiah (balconies) is near the Coptic Convent, is on the street called Street of the Patriarchs leading out of Street of David. From platform in front of my chamber, command view of battered dome of Church of Sepulchre & Mount Olivet. Opposite house is open space, ruins of old Latin Convent, destroyed by some enemy centuries ago & never since rebuilt. Landlord pointed out the damaged dome, as beginning of the war with Russia. Still in same state as then. Walked out to the North of the city, but my eyes so affected by the long days ride in the glare of the light of arid hills, had to come back to hotel.

Jan 7th All day with the dragoman roaming over the hills.

Jan 8th The same.

Jan 9th. Thought I should have been the only stranger in Jerusalem, but this afternoon came over from Jaffa, a Mr Frederich Cunningham, of Boston, a very prepossessing young man who seemed rejoiced to meet a companion & countryman.

Jan 10th (Some mistake in my dates, but which I

[1]This hotel reappears in *Clarel*, Vol. 1, p. 7; and in Murray's *Handbook for Travellers in Syria and Palestine* (1858), warning is given of its damp rooms, and that "complaints have been made too of the state of its cuisine, and the *long bills* made up for extras."

cant now rectify.) Spent the remaining days till Jan. 18th in roaming about city & visiting Jordan & Dead Sea.

Jan 19th. Quitted Jerusalem with Mr Cunningham & his dragoman—the Druze,[1] Abdallah—Stayed at Greek convent at Ramlah. No sleep. Old monk like rat. Scurvy treatment. Letter from Greek Patriarch.[2] Countess staying there.—Before going to convent visited the ruined mosque (?) & tower of Ramlah.[3] A curious sight.

Jan 20th Rode from Ramlah to Lydda. A robbery of a village near by, by party of Arabs, alarms the whole country. People travel in bands. We rode to Lydda in train of the Governor's son. A mounted escort of some 30 men, all armed. Fine riding. Musket-shooting. Curvetting & caracoling of the horsemen. Outriders. Horsemen riding to one side, scorning the perils. Riding up to hedges of cactus, interrogating & firing their pistols into them. Entering Lydda, Governor's son discharged all his barrels (revolver) into a puddle—& we went to

[1]The Druze guide in *Clarel* first appears for a full-length portrait Vol. 1, p. 197. He continues in the back-ground nearly to the end of the poem.

[2]Which also turns up again in *Clarel*, Vol. 2, p. 46.

[3]Melville was right; it was the "White Mosque," the oldest in Ramlah, famous for the view from its minaret, but with its original summit lost.

see the ruined church of Lydda. Evidently of the time of the Crusades. A delightful ride across Plain of Sharon to Jaffa. Quantities of red poppies. (Rose of Sharon?)[1] Found the *Petra Party*[2] at Jaffa. In the afternoon had a bath in the Meditteranean. Inspected some old ruins of walls by & in, the sea. *Jan 22d* Mr Cunningham & the Petra party left this afternoon in the French steamer for Alexandria. Very rough getting off. After their departure, returned to the place called "the hotel," and ascended to the top of the house—the only promenade in the town.—Jaffa is situated upon a hill rising steeply from the sea, & sloping away inland towards the Plain of Sharon. It is walled & garrisoned. The houses, old, dark, arched & vaulted, and of stone. The house I sojourn in crowns the summit of the hill, & is the highest from the ground of any. From the top of it, I see the Mediterranean, the Plain, the mountains of Ephraim. A lovely landscape. To the North the nearest spot is Beyroot; to the South, Gaza—that Phillistine city the gates of which Sampson shouldered.—I am the

[1]*Clarel*, Vol. 1, p. 4:

And was it, yes, her titled Rose,
That scarlet poppy oft at hand?

[2]This party which had been down in Arabia to view the ruins of Petra evidently regaled Melville with the wonders of the place, as witness *Clarel*, Part 2, Canto 30: *Of Petra.*

only traveller sojourning in Jaffa. I am emphatically alone, & begin to feel like Jonah.[1] The wind is rising, the swell of the sea increasing, & dashing in breakers upon the reef of rocks within a biscuit's toss of the sea-wall. The surf shows a great sheet of yeast along the beach—N & S, far as eye can reach.

Jan 23d Could not sleep last night for the fleas. Rose early & to top of the house. The wind & sea still high. No boat could get off in this weather. Wrote in this diary (Jerusalem) today. In the afternoon called upon Mr & Mrs Saunders, outside the wall, the American Missionary.—Dismal story of their experiments. Might as well attempt to convert bricks into bride-cake as the Orientals into Christians. It is against the will of God that the East should be Christianized. Mrs S, an interesting woman, not without beauty, and of the heroine stamp, or desires to be. A book lying on her table, entitled "Book of Female Heroines", I took to be the exponent of her aspirations. She talked to me, alone, for two hours; I doing nothing but listen.

[1]It will be remembered that when Jonah "rose up to flee into Tarshish from the presence of the Lord he went down to Jaffa and found a ship and paid the fare; but the Lord hurled a great wind into the sea." And in this connection, Father Mapple's immortal sermon in *Moby-Dick* should be read again.

Mr S. came in. A man feeble by Nature & feebler by sickness; but worthy. A Seventh Day Baptist—God help him! A Miss Williams, an elderly English woman, a kind of religious teacher, joined us in a walk through the orange groves.

Jan 24th No sleep last night—only resource to cut tobacco & watch the six windows of my room, which is like a light-house—& hear the surf & wind. The genuine Jonah feeling, in Jaffa too, is worth experiencing in the same sense that, according to Byron, the murderer sensations were worth a trial.—Jaffa is certainly antedeluvian—a port before the Flood. It has no antiquities worth speaking of.—It is too ancient. Yet I have been to the alleged home of Simon the Tanner—"by the sea" & with a wall. It is now the site of a mosque & shrine. I have such a feeling in this lonely old Jaffa, with the prospect of a prolonged detention here, owing to the surf—that it is only by stern self-control & grim defiance that I contrive to keep cool & patient.—The main beam crossing my chamber overhead, is evidently taken from a wreck—the trenail holes proving it.[1] In the right lintel of the

[1]*Clarel*, Vol. 1, p. 91:

A hermitage how confortless.
The beams of the low ceiling bare
Were wreck-stuff from the Joppa strand."

door is a vial masoned in, & . . . . ,[1] containing some text of Jewish scripture—a charm. The keeper of the place is a Jew.[2] All of which proves the old —genuine, old Jonah feeling.

Jan 25th [*Friday*] Thank God got some sleep last night. Wind & sea subsided. Lovely day, but wet underfoot. The showers yesterday towards evening were like our June showers.—Walked on top of the house. Read Dumas's "Diamond Necklace"[3]—Excellent, Cagliostro's talk in opening chapter.—Walked out & looked at rocks before the town. After dinner went with Mr Saunders to Mr Dickson's.

Jan 26th Saturday—Bravo!—This moment, sitting down to jot a while, hear that the Austrian Steamer is in sight, & going to the window, beheld her.—Thus then will end nearly six days in Jaffa.—This morning very clear, & from the house-top I think

[1]Illegible.

[2]*Clarel*, Vol. 1, p. 9:

A lamp whose sidelong rays are shed
On a slim vial set in bed
Of door-post all of masonry.
    That vial hath the Gentile vexed;
Within it holds Talmudic text
Or charm. And there the Black Jew sits,
Abdon the host.

[3]*Le collier de la reine.*

I see Lebanon—Mt Hermon,[1] it may be—for its summit is covered with snow.—11. A. M. Just returned from stroll. Steamer drawing nigh. Was again pleased with the queer school kept in chicken-coop under dim arches nigh Gate. Old Turk schoolmaster, smoking away solemn as ever.—Took boat & rowed off to rocks off harbor. They bear no appearance, as some affirm, of being ruins of an ancient pier, (☞ Jonah's pier) or any ruins of any work of art. It is the remnant of a rocky ledge, worn away into *seeming* ruins of old piers, by continual wear of the sea. At a little distance, the rock looks to be mere dirt-heaps, being of same color. But in fact are excessively hard & tough. Some look igneus. While by the water saw men emptying sacks of rubbish into the harbor, such as it is. Vastly improving, this.—Amused with the autographs & confessions of people who have stayed at this hotel. "I have *existed* at this hotel &c &c." Something comical could be made out of all this. Let the confessions being of a religious, penitential resigned & ambiguous turn, apparently flattering to the host, but really derogatory to the place.—Bright sun & sea. You seem to look through a vaccum at everything. The sea is like a great daub of Prussian blue.

[1] In pencil, above the line: (*Not so—a mistake*).

From Jerusalem to Dead Sea &c[1]

Over Olivet by St: Stephens Gate to Bethany—on a hill—wretched Arab village—fine view—Tomb of Lazarus, a mere cave or cell—On down into vallies & over hills—all barren—Brook Kedron—immense depth—black & funereal—Valley of Jehosophat, grows more diabolical as approaches Dead Sea—Plain of Jerico—looks green, (part of it), an orchard, but only trees of apple of Sodom—P. of J. corresponds to P. of S. on other side of mountains. Mount of Temptation—a black, arid mount—nought to be seen but Dead Sea, mouth of Kedron—very tempting—foolish feind—but it was a display in vision—then why take him up to Mount?—the *thing itself* was in vision.—Where Kedron opens into Plain of Jerico looks like Gate of Hell.—Tower with sheiks smoking & huts on top—thick walls—village of Jerico—ruins on hill-side—tent—fine dinner—jolly time—sitting at door

[1]Part 2 of *Clarel*, entitled *The Wilderness* parallels closely this pilgrimage that follows. I have not cluttered the page with detailed cross-references, though I have minutely compared the two accounts.

of tent looking at Mountains of Moab.—tent the charmed circle, keeping off the curse. Marsaba.[1]—Rain at night—Thunder in mountains of Moab—Lightning—cries of jackall & wolf.—Broke up camp—rain—wet—rode out on *mouldy* plains—nought grows but wiry, prickly bush—muddy—every creature *in human form* seen ahead—escort alarmed & galloped on to learn something—salutes—every man understands it—shows native dignity—worthy of salute—Arabs on hills over Jordan—alarm—scampering ahead of escort—after rain, turbid & yellow streams—foliaged banks—beyond, arid hills.—Arabs crossing the river—lances—old crusaders — pistols — menacing cries — tobacco.—Robbers—rob Jerico annually—&c—Ride over mouldy plain to Dead Sea—Mountains on . . . . .[2] side—Lake George[3]—all but verdure.—foam on beach & pebbles like slaver of mad dog—smarting bitter of the water,—carried the bitter in my mouth all day—bitterness of life—thought of all bitter things—Bitter is it to be poor & bitter, to be reviled, & Oh bitter are these waters of Death, thought I.—Old boughs tossed up by water—relics of pick-nick—nought to eat but bitumen & ashes

[1]A monastery, and the scene of *Clarel:* Part 3.
[2]Illegible.
[3]In pencil, *Como* is substituted. See *Clarel*, Vol. 1, p. 292.

with desert of Sodom apples washed down with water of Dead Sea. [Rainbow over Dead Sea—heaven, after all, has no malice against it.][1]—Must bring your own provisions, as well, too for mind, as body—for all is barren. Drank of brook, but brackish.—Ascended among the mountains again—barren.—

Barrenness of Judea[2]

Whitish mildew pervading whole tracts of land-scape—bleached—leprosy—encrustation of curses—old cheese—bones of rocks,—crunched, knawed, & mumbled[3]—mere refuse & rubbish of creation—like that laying outside of Jaffa Gate—all Judea seems to have been accumulations of this rubbish.—So rubbishy, that no chiffonier could find anything all over it.—No moss as in other ruins—no grace of decay—no ivy—the unleavened nakedness of desolation—whitish ashes—lime-kilns—You see the anatomy—compares with ordinary regions as skeleton with living & rosy man.—

[1]Along the right margin. This rainbow reappears in *Clarel*, Vol I, p. 295.

[2]This is the predominant note in *Clarel*.

[3]The reading is strange enough, but so the text seems to say. In *Clarel*, Vol. I, p. 292, this becomes: "Charred or crunched or riven."

Port Esquiline of the Universe[1] (For Note).

St. Saba—Samphire gatherers—Monks dreadful trade.[2]

[1]*Clarel*, Vol. 1, p. 97, gives almost vicious point to this.
Like ancient Rome's port Esquiline
Wherefrom the scum was cast.—

[2]The reference is of course to *Lear* IV, VI:
half way down
Hangs one that gathers samphire, dreadful trade!

Cf. *Clarel*, Vol. 2, p. 43, at Mar Saba:
Aloof the monks their aerie keep,
Down from their hanging cells they peep,
Like samphire-gatherers o'er the bay.

[1]Crossed elevated plains, with snails, (and)[2] tracks of slime, all over—shut in by ashy hills—wretched sheep & black goats.—Arab—Bedouin encampment in hollow of high hills—oval—like two rows of hearses—Brook Kedron—two branches—*St. Saba* —zig-zag along Kedron, sepulchral ravine, smoked as by fire, caves & & cells—immense depth—all rock—enigma of the depth—rain only two or 3 days a year—wall of stone on ravine edge—Monastery (Greek) rode on with letter—hauled up in basket into hole—small door of massive iron in high wall—knocking—opened—salaam of monks—Place for pilgrims—divans—St Saba wine—"racka"—comfortable.—At dusk went down by many stone steps & through mysterious passages to cave & trap doors & hole in wall—ladder—ledge after ledge—winding—to bottom of Brook Kedron—sides of ravine all caves of recluses—Monastery a congregation of stone eyries, enclosed with wall—Good bed & night's rest—Went into chapel &c—little hermitage in rock—balustrades of iron—

[1]This section is the skeleton of the second volume of *Clarel:* Part 3—*Mar Saba*, and Part 4—*Bethlehem.*

[2]I have substituted this for a word I cannot decipher. Cf. *Clarel*, Vol. 2, p. 36:

A moor of chalk or slimy clay,
With gluey track and streaky trail
Of some small slug or torpid snail.

lonely monks.—black-birds—feeding with herd—numerous terraces, balconies—solitary Date Palm mid-way in precipice—Good bye—Over lofty hills to Bethlehem.—on a hill—old chapel of Helena—(Passed over Bethlehem hills where shepherds were watching their flocks, (as of old) but a Moslem with back to Jerusalem (face to Mecca) praying.—In chapel, monk (Latin) took us down into cave after cave,—tomb of saints—lights burning (with olive oil) till came to place of Nativity (many lamps) & manger with lights. View from roof of chapel &c.—Ride to Jerusalem—pressing forward to save the rain.—On way to Bethlehem saw Jerusalem from distance—unless knew it, could not have recognized it—looked exactly like arid rocks See page *124* of SAUNDERS[1] for curious description of Jerusalem.[2]

☞ (Jerusalem Cross 5. Wounds)[2]

P. 124.

[1]I have examined the title of every book written by any Saunders in all available library catalogues, but I can find no title that seems appropriate to this reference.

[2]In pencil, at bottom of the page.

Jerusalem[1]

Village of Lepers—houses facing the wall—Zion. Their park, a dung-heap.—They sit by the gates asking alms,—then whine—avoidance of them & horror.
Ghostliness of the names—Jehosophat—Hermon &c.
Thoughts in the Via Dolorosa—women panting under burdens—men with melancholy faces.
Wandering among the tombs—till I began to think myself one of the possessed with devils.
Variety of the Tombs—with stairs like pulpit &c. "Multitudes, multitudes" in the Valley of Hermon. (tradition authorized by Scripture) Stones about Absalom's Tomb—grave-stones about Zachariah's.
Church of Holy Sepulchre. Broken dome—anointing stone—lamps—dingy,—queer smell—irregular—caves—grots—Chapel of Friends of the Cross. Pilgrims—chatting—poor—resting
Armenian Convent—Large—pilgrims.
Hill—side view of Zion—loose stones & gravel as if shot down from carts.
[The mind cannot but be sadly & suggestively affected with the indifference of Nature & Man to all

[1]*Clarel, Part I—Jerusalem,* amplifies this section. In the other three parts of the poem, however, where Jerusalem is discussed in retrospect, portions of this section are elaborated.

that makes the spot sacred to the Christian. Weeds grow upon Mount Zion; side by side in impartiality[1] appear the shadows of church & mosque, and on Olivet every morning the sun indifferently ascends over the Chapel of the Ascension.

[The South East angle of wall. Mosque of Omar—Solomon's Temple. Here the wall of Omar rises upon the foundation stones of Solomon, triumphing over that which sustains it, an emblem of the relationship of the two faiths.

[How it affects one to be cheated in Jerusalem.

[2][The old Connecticut man wandering about with tracts &c—knew not the language.—hopelessness of it—his lonely batchelor rooms—he maintained that the expression "Oh Jerusalem!" was an argument proving that Jerusalem was a byeword &c.

[Warder Crisson of Philadelphia—An American turned Jew—divorced from former wife—married a Jewess &c—Sad.

[The strange arches, cisterns, &c you come upon about Jerusalem—every day discovered something new in this way.

[Siloam—pool, hill, village. (Here, at narrow gorge

[1]*Equality*, above the line.

[2]"The Sinner Nehemiah," who figures so largely in *Clarel* is undoubtedly a closely studied portrait of this "flitting tract dispensing man."

begins Vale of Kedron &c. Village, occupying the successive terraces of tombs excavated in the perpendicular faces of living rock. Living occupants of the tombs—household arrangements. One used for an oven. Others for granaries.—

[In Jehosophat, Jew graves stones lie as if indiscriminately flung abroad by a blast in a quarry. So thick, a warren of the dead—so old, the Hebrew inscriptions can hardly be distinguished from the wrinkles formed by Time. Shapeless stones &c.—(See over leaf) Side by side here tombs of Absolom, Zachariah & St James. Cut out of live rock in Petra style. St: James a stone verandah overlooking the gorge-pillars.—Jehosophat, shows seams of natural rock—capitals of pilasters rubbed off by Time.—Large hole in front—full of stones inside, heap of stones (cart loads) before it—The maledictory contribution of the pilgrims, one of the melancholy amenities of Jerusalem. (See Bible for origin of Tombs) To be stoned is his memorial.—The grave stones project *out* from the side-hill, as if already in act of resurrection. At distance hardly tell them from natural rock which lies profusely around. The stones climb mid-way up Olivet. Opposite, the cemetery of the Turks—close up to walls of the city, & barring the way of the closed arches of the Beautiful Gate.—(Christ sitting in window)[1]—both Jew & Turk sleeping in another faith than that of Him who ascended from the nigh Olivet.—The city beseiged by army of the dead.—cemeteries all round.—

[The Beautiful, or Golden, Gate — two arches, highly ornamental sculpture, undoubtedly old, Herod's time—the gate from which Christ would go to Bethany & Olivet—& also that in which he made is entry (with palms) into the city. Turks walled it up because of tradition that through this Gate the city would be taken.—One of the most interesting things in Jerusalem—seems expressive of the finality of Christianity, as if this was the last religion of the world,—no other, possible.

[In pursuance of my object, the saturation of my mind with the atmosphere of Jerusalem, offering myself up a passive subject, and no unwilling one, to its weird[2] impressions, I always rose at dawn & walked without the walls. Nor so far as escaping the pent-up air within, was concerned was I singular here.

For daily I could not but be struck with the clusters of the townspeople reposing along the arches near the Jaffa Gate where it looks down into the Vale of Gihon, and the groups always haunting

[1]In pencil, above the line, and unintelligible to me.

[2]Substituted for *melancholy*, which is crossed out.

the neighboring fountains, vales & hills. They too seemed to feel the insalubriousness of so small a city pent in by lofty walls obstructing ventilation, postponing the morning & hastening the unwholesome twilight. And they too seemed to share my impatience[1] were it only at this arbitrary limitation & prescription of things.—I would stroll to Mount Zion, along the terraced walks, & survey the tomb stones of the hostile Armenians, Latins, Greeks, all sleeping together.—I looked along the hill side of Gihon over against me, & watched the precipitation of the solemn shadows of the city towers flung far down to the bottom of the pool of Gihon, and higher up the haunted darkened valley my eye rested on the cliff-girt basin, haggard with riven old olives, where the angel of the Lord smote the army of Sennacherib. (Hill of Evil Counsel) And smote by the morning I saw the reddish soil of Aceldama, confessing its inexpiable guilt by deeper dyes. On the Hill of Evil Counsel, I saw the ruined villa of the High Priest where tradition says the death of Christ was plotted, and the field where when all was over the traitor Judas hung himself. [And in the afternoon, I would stand out by St Stephen's Gate, Nigh the pool likewise named after him, occupying the spot where he was stoned, and

[1]Doubtful reading.

watch the shadows slowly sliding (sled-like) down the hills of Berotha & Zion into the valley of Jehosophat, then after resting a while in the bottom of the ravine, slowly begin creeping up the opposite side of Olivet, entering tomb after tomb & cave after cave. &c.—Pilgrims, their serious expressions, wandering about the hills &c.—

[The Holy Sepulchre—(No Jew allowed in church of H.S.)[1]—ruined dome—confused & half-ruinous pile.—Labyrinths & terraces of mouldy grottos, tombs, & shrines. Smells like a dead-house. Dingy light.—At the entrance, in a sort of grotto in the wall a divan for Turkish policemen, where they sit cross legged & smoking, scornfully observing the continuous troops of pilgrims entering & prostrating themselves before the anointing-stone of Christ, which veined with shreds of a mouldy red looks like a butcher's slab.—Near by is a blind stair of worn marble, ascending to the reputed Calvary where among other (things the showman point show)[2] you by the smoky light of old pawnbrokers lamps of dirty gold, the hole in which the cross was fixed and through a baker's grating as

[1]In pencil, between the lines.

[2]Melville first wrote: *things they show you;* then he inserted above the line, after *things*, *the showman point*, and crossed out *they*. The sense is clear if not the grammar.

over a coal-cellar, point out the rent in the rock![1] On the same level, nearby is a kind of gallery, railed with marble, overlooking the entrance of the church; and here almost every day I would hang looking down upon the spectacle of the scornful Turks on the divan, & the scorned pilgrims kissing the stone of the anointing.—The door of the church is like that of a jail—a grated window in it.—The main body of the church is overhung by the lofty & ruinous dome whose fallen plastering reveals the meagre skeleton of beams & laths. A sort of plague-stricken splendor reigns in the painted & mildewed walls around. In the midst of all, stands the Sepulchre; a church in a church. It is of marble, richly sculptured in parts & bearing the faded aspect of age. From its porch, issue a garish steam of light upon the faces of the pilgrims who crowd for admittance into a space which will hold but four or five at a time. First passing a wee[2] vestibule where is shown the stone on which the angel sat, you enter the tomb. It is like entering a lighted coffin. Wedged & half-dazzled, you stare for a moment on the ineloquence of the bedizened slab, and

[1]Along the right margin, in crayon, and underscored: *Greek tickets for Heaven. See Captain's story.* The Captain's story is given later, on p. 108.

[2]This reading may be questioned; but Melville uses *wee* several times in *Clarel*.

glad to come out, wipe your brow glad to escape as from the heat & jam of a show-box. All is glitter & nothing is gold. A sickening cheat. The countenances of the poorest & most ignorant pilgrims would seem tacitly to confess it as well as your own.

After being but a little while in the church, going the rapid round of the chapels & shrines, they either stand still in listless disappointment, or seat themselves in huddles about the numerous stairways, indifferently exchanging the sectarian gossip of the day. The Church of the Sepulcre is the thronged news-room & theological exchange of Jerusalem, and still the more appears so, from various little chapels, the special property of the minor sects of the Copts, the Syrians & others, which here & there beneath the dome meet the eye, much like those boxes of stock-auctioneers,[1] which one sees in commercial Exchanges.—The Chapel of the Friends of the Cross.—wine cellar &c. —If you approach the church from the squalid alley leading towards it from the Via Dolorosa, you pass a long old wall, lofty & dingy, in every corner of whose massive buttresses at their base, lie in open exposure an accumulation of the last & least nameable filth of a barbarous city. But at the time you are far from imagining that the wall treated with

[1]Questionable reading.

such affront continually (by the Turks, only, it is to be hoped) is a main wall of the fabric containing the supposed tomb of one of the persons of the Godhead. This wall passed, you dive into a steep wynd, like those in Edinburgh, and presently come to a space less confined, where you are met by a thick wall fenced by a paling with an old wooden gate, low enough & grimy enough to be the entrance to a stye. This admits you to the immediate masonry-locked court of the Church. A considerable area, flagged with ....[1] stones, upon which are seated a multitude of hawkers & pedlers of rosaries, crucifixes, toys of olive wood and Dead Sea stone, & various other amulets & charms. The front of the Church is made very irregular, by the careless lapping over of subsequent erections upon the original one. To the left is a high & .....[1] tower, which like an aged pine, is barked at bottom, & all decay at top. Much elaborate sculpture once graced what is now visible of the original facade; but Time has nibbled it away, till it now looks like so much spoiled pastry at which the mice have been at work. INTERIOR OF JERUSALEM. Leads from St. Stephens Gate up towards Calvary. Silence & solitude of it. The arch—the stone he leaned against—the stone of Lazarus &c. City like a quarry—all stone.—

[1]Illegible.

Vaulted ways—buttresses (flying) Arch (Ecce homo). Some one has built a little batchelor's abode on top. *Talk of the guides.* "Here is the stone Christ leaned against, & here is the English Hotel." Yonder is the arch where Christ was shown to the people, & just by that open window is sold the best coffee in Jerusalem. &c &c &c.

[Had Jerusalem no peculiar historic associations, still would it, by its physical aspect evoke peculiar emotion in the traveller. [As the sight of haunted Haddon Hall suggested to Mrs Radcliffe her curdling romances, so I have little doubt, the diabolical[1] landscape of Judea must have suggested to the Jewish prophets, their ghastly[2] theology.

[Wearily climbing the Via Dolorosa one noon I heard the muezzin calling to prayer from the mineret of Omar. He does the same from that of Mt. Olivet.

[The olive tree much resembles in its grotesque contortions the apple tree—only it is much more gnarled & less lively in its green. It is generally planted in orchards, which helps the resemblance. It is a haunted melancholy looking tree (sober & penitent), quite in keeping with Jerusalem & its associations. There are many olives on the plain north of the walls. The Cave of Jeremiah is in this

[1]Alternately Melville crossed out *haunted, horrible.*
[2]Arrived at after discarding *diabolical, terrible, terrific.*

part. In its lamentable recesses he composed his lamentable lamentations.

[Inside the walls are many vacant spaces, overgrown with the horrible cactus.

[The color of the whole city is grey & looks at you like a cold grey eye in a cold old man.—its strange aspect in the pale olive light of the morning.

[There are *strata* of cities buried under the present surface of Jerusalem. Forty feet deep lie fragments of columns &c.

[Stones of Judea. We read a good deal about stones in Scriptures. (Stories of these)[1] Monuments & memorials are set up of stones; men are stoned to death; the figurative seed falls in stony places; and no wonder that stones should so largely figure in the Bible. Judea is one accumulation of stones—Stony mountains & stony plains; stony torrents & stony roads; stony vales & stony fields, stony homes & stony tombs; (stony eyes & stony hearts).[2] Before you, & behind you are stones. Stones to right & stones to left. In many places laborious attempts have been made, to clear the surface of these stones. You see heaps of stones here & there; and stone walls of immense thickness are thrown together, less for boundries than to get them out of

[1]Above the line.

[2]Crossed out, and then restored.

the way. But in vain; The removal of one stone only serves to reveal those stones still lying, below it. It is like mending the old barn; the more you uncover, the more it grows.—The toes of every ones shoes are all stubbed to pieces with the stones. They are seldom a round . . . .[1] stone; but sharp, flinty & scratchy. But in the roads, such as that to Jaffa, they have been worn smooth by continuous travel.—To account for the abundance of stones, many theories have been stated; *My* theory is that long ago, some whimsical King of the country took it into his head to pave all Judea, and entered into contracts to that effect; but the contractor becoming bankrupt mid-way in his business, the stones were only dumped on the ground, & there they lie to this day [There is some prophecy about the highways being prepared for the coming of the Jews and when the "deputation from the Scotch Church" were in Judea, they suggested to Sir Moses Montefiore the expediency of employing the poorer sort of Jews in this work—at the same time facilitating prophecy and clearing the *stones* out of the way.

The hills. Are stones in the concrete. Regular layers of rock; some ampitheatres disposed in seats, & terraces. The stone walls (loose) seem not the erec-

[1]Illegible.

tions of art, but mere natural varieties of the stony landscape. In some of the fields, lie large grotesque rocks—all perforated & honey combed—like rotting bones of mastadons.—Everything looks old. Compared with these rocks, those in Europe or America look juvenile.

Caves. Judea honey combed with them. No wonder that these gloomy (caves)[1] became retreat of tens of thousands of gloomy anchorites.

[There is at all times a smell of burning rubbish in the air of Jerusalem.

[The so-called pool of Bethseda full of rubbish.—sooty look & smell.

[Three Sundays a week in Jerusalem—Jew, Christian, Turk. And now comes the missionaries of the 7th Day Baptists, & add a fourth. (Saturday—the Jews)—How it must puzzle the converts!

[The road from Jaffa to Jerusalem in parts very wide & full of separate divergent foot-paths, worn by the multitude of pilgrims of divergent faiths.

[Arabs plowing in their shirt-tails. Some of them old men. Old age is venerable,—but hardly in the shirt tail.

[Part of Jerusalem built on quarries—entrance from North wall.

[No country will more quickly dissipate romantic

[1]Omitted in the manuscript.

expectations than Palestine—particularly Jerusalem. To some the disappointment is heart sickening. &c.

[Is the desolation of the land the result of the fatal embrace of the Deity? Hapless are the favorites of Heaven.

[In the emptiness of the lifeless antiquity of Jerusalem the emigrant Jews are like flies that have taken up their abode in a skull.

Christian Missions &c in Palestine & Syria

A great deal of money has been spent by the *English Mission in Jerusalem.* Church on Mt Zion estimated to have cost $75,000. It is a fine edifice. The present Bishop (Gobat,[1] a Swiss by birth) seems a very sincere man, and doubtless does his best. (Long ago he was 3 years in Abyssinia. His Journal is published.[2] Written in a strikingly unaffected style—apostolically concise & simple.) But the work over which he presides in Jerusalem is a failure—palpably. One of the missionaries under Gobat confessed to Mrs. Saunders that out of all the Jew converts, but one he believed to be a true Christian,—with much more. All kinds of variance of opinion & jealousies prevail. The same man

[1]The Rev. Samuel Gobat arrived in Jerusalem in 1846. Though Bishop of Palestine, Syria, Egypt and Mesopotamia, he had but one parish in his diocese—Jerusalem, with less than fifty communicants. Outside Jerusalem, his task, therefore, was to create a protestant people.

[2]His *Journal of Three Years' Residence in Abyssinia* was published in 1850.

mentioned above also said to Mrs S. many things tending to the impression that the Mission was as full of intrigues as a ward-meeting or caucus at home.
I often passed the Protestant School &c on Mt Zion, but nothing seemed going on. The only place of interest there was the Grave Yard. I attended a Missionary meeting in Jerusalem (to raise money for some other far-away place) but was not specially edified. In a year's time they have raised for "foreign missions" about £3,10, or something of that sort.
At Smyrna The American Mission is discontinued. The sorriest accounts were given me there. No one converted but with a carnal end in view on part of convert.
At Jaffa, Mr & Mrs Saunders from Rhode-Island. Mr Saunders a broken-down machinist & returned Californian out at elbows. Mrs. S a superior woman in many respects. They were sent out to found an Agricultural School for the Jews. They tried it but miserably failed. The Jews would come, pretend to be touched & all that, get clothing & then—vanish. Mrs S. said they were very "deceitful". Mr S. now does nothing—health gone by climate. Mrs S. learning Arabic from a Sheik, & turned doctress to the poor. She is waiting the Lord's time, she says. For this she is well qualified, being of great patience. Their little girl looks sickly &

pines for home[1]—but the Lord's work must be done. *Mrs Minot of Philadelphia*—came out some 3 or four (years)[2] ago to start a kind of Agricultural Academy for Jews. She seems to have been the first person actively to engage in this business, and by her pen incited others. A woman of fanatic energy & spirit. After a short stay at Jaffa, she returned to America for contributions; succeeded in the attempt & returned with implements, money &c. Bought a tract about a mile & half from Jaffa. Two young ladies came out with her from America. They had troubles. Not a single Jew was converted either to Christianity or Agriculture. The young ladies sickened & went home. A month afterwards, Mrs Minot died,—I passed her place. *Deacon Dickson of Groton, Mass.* This man caught the contagion from Mrs Minot's published letters. Sold his farm at home & came out with wife, son & three daughters, about two years ago.—Be it said, that all these movements combining Agriculture & Religion in reference to Palestine, are based upon the impression (Mrs Minot's & other's) that the time for the prophetic return of the Jews

[1]Cf. *Clarel*, Vol. I, p. 108:

> Ruth, too, when here a child she came,
> Would blurt in reckless childhood's way,
> " 'Tis a bad place."

[2]Omitted in the manuscript.

to Judea is at hand, and therefore the way must be prepared for them by Christians, both in setting them right in their faith & their farming—in other words, preparing the soil literally & figuratively.—With Mr Saunders I walked out to see Mr Dickson's place. About an hour from Jaffa Gate. The house & enclosure were like the ordinary ones of the better class of Arabs. Some twelve acres were under cultivation. Mulberry trees, oranges, pomegranates,—wheat, barley, tomatoes &c.—On the Plain of Sharon, in view of mountain of Ephraim.—Mr Dickson a thorough Yankee, about 60, with long Oriental beard, blue Yankee coat, & Shaker waistcoat.—At the house we were ushered into a comfortless—barn-yard sort of apartment & introduced to Mrs D. a respectable looking elderly woman. We took chairs. After some introductory remarks the following talk ensued—

H.M. "Have you settled here permanently, Mr Dickson?"

Mr D. "Permanently settled on the soil of Zion, Sir." with a kind of dogged emphasis.

Mrs. D (as if she dreaded her husband's getting on his hobby, & was pained by it)—"The walking is a little muddy, aint it?"— (This to Mr S.)

H.M. to Mr D. "Have you any Jews working with you?"

Mr D. No. Can't afford to have them. Do my own work, with my son. Besides, the Jews are lazy & dont like work.

H.M. "And do you not think that a hindrance to making farmers of them?"

Mr D. "That's it. The Gentile Christians must teach them better. The fact is the fullness of Time has come. The Gentile Christians must prepare the way.

Mrs D. (to me) "Sir, is there in America a good deal of talk about Mr D's efforts here?

Mr D. Yes, do they believe basically[1] in the restoration of the Jews?

H. M. I can't really answer that.

Mrs D. I suppose most people believe the propheseys to that effect in a figurative sense—dont they?

H M. Not unlikely. &c&c&c.

They have two daughters married here to Germans, & living near, fated to beget a progeny of hybrid vagabonds.—Old Dickson seems a man of Puritanic energy, and being inoculated with this preposterous Jew mania, is resolved to carry his Quixotism through to the end. Mrs D. dont seem to like it, but submits,—The whole thing is half melancholy, half farcical—like all the rest of the world.

[1]Tentative reading.

Dr Kayok (?)[1] *English Consul.* This gentleman, born in the Levant, was some years in England. He awakened great interest there in behalf of the Jews, and came to Joppa at last to start some missionary project, and was not unprovided with funds contributed by the pious in England.—Long since he gave up the whole project, engaged in trade, is now a flourishing man, & English Consul. At any hints in reference to Missions, he betrays aversion to converse. It is whispered that he was someway trickish with the funds.

Sir Joseph Montefiore. This Croesus visited Palestine last year, bought a large tract on the hill of Gihon & walled it in for hospital grounds. A huge man of 75, he was carried to Jerusalem from Joppa, on a litter borne by mules. They fleeced him sadly, charging enormous prices for everything he bought. Sir J. seems to have the welfare of his poor countrymen near his heart, and it is said purposes returning, here for life.—

The idea of making farmers of the Jews is vain.

[1]The interrogation is Melville's, and I have been unable to settle the doubt. Murray's *Handbook for Travellers in Syria and Palestine*, 1858 (p. 287), seems contemptuously to with-hold the name. It says: "[Jaffa] has been needlessly honoured with an English consul; for except to be sent out of the way, or to make money, it will be difficult to discern what a consul has to do here."

In the first place, Judea is a desert with few exceptions. In the second place, the Jews hate farming. All who cultivate the soil in Palestine are Arabs. The Jews dare not live outside walled towns or villages for fear of the malicious persecution of the Arabs & Turks.—Besides, the number of Jews in Palestine is comparatively small. And how are the hosts of them scattered in other lands to be brought here? Only by a miracle.

Strange revelation made to me by Mr Wood (of Concord N.H) American Consul at Beyroot, concerning hidden life of Mrs Minot. Considered by him & L. Napier as crazy woman. Also about Miss Williams—Campbellite &c.

Mr Wood saw Mr Dickson going about Jerusalem with open Bible, looking for the opening asunder of Mount Olivet and the preparing of the highway for the Jews. &c

(Arch of Ecce Homo) [1]

[1]This, in pencil, Melville added as a coda. The thirteenth canto of the first part of *Clarel* is entitled *The Arch.* And from this I must quote at length as evidence of the passionate and embittered disillusionment with which Melville came to view Christianity.

> No raptures which with saints prevail,
> Nor trouble of compunction born
> He felt, as there he seemed to scan
> Aloft in spectral guise, the pale
> Still face, the purple robe, and thorn;

And inly cried—*Behold the Man!*
Yon Man it is this burden lays:
Even he who in the pastoral hours,
Abroad in fields, and cheered by flowers,
Announced a heaven's unclouded days;
And, ah, with such persuasive lips—
Those lips now sealed while doom delays—
Won men to look for solace there;
But, crying out in death's eclipse,
When rainbow none his eyes might see,
Enlarged the margin for despair—
My God, my God, forsakest me?

Upbraider! we upbraid again;
Thee we upbraid; our pangs constrain
Pathos itself to cruelty.
Ere yet thy day no pledge was given
Of homes and mansions in the heaven—
Paternal homes reserved for us;
Heart hoped it not, but lived content—
Content with life's own discontent,
Nor deemed that fate ere swerved for us:
The natural law men let prevail;
Then reason disallowed the state
Of instinct's variance with fate.
But thou—ah, see, in rack how pale
Who did the world with throes convulse;
Behold him—yea—behold the Man
Who warranted if not began
The dream that drags out its repulse.

Nature and thee in vain we search:
Well urged the Jews within the porch—
"How long wilt make us still to doubt?"

How long?—'Tis eighteen cycles now—
Enigma and evasion grow;
And shall we never find thee out?
What isolation lones thy state
That all we else know cannot mate
With what thou teachest?
                                        By what art
Of conjuration might the heart
Of heavenly love, so sweet, so good,
Corrupt into the creeds malign,
Begetting strife's pernicious brood,
Which claimed for patron thee divine?

    Anew, anew,
For this thou bleedest, Anguished Face;
Yea, thou through ages to accrue,
Shalt the Medusa shield replace:
In beauty and in terror too
Shalt paralyze the nobler race—
Smite or suspend, perplex, deter—
Tortured, shalt prove a torturer.

Jan 27th Got on board the Austrian steamer "Aquile Imperiale" at I. P. M. yesterday, but did not sail till late in the evening. Much wind & sea all night. In morning coast in view,—Lebanon Mountains—snow-topped—Mt Hermon not in sight—inland.—At 2. P. M came to anchor at Beyroot.—Hotel Bel View—dragoman to Warburton—Sirocco blowing. Town occupies tongue of land projecting from base of Leabanon. Lofty mountains all round. Walled town. Old ruins of Castles of Crusaders. Town between desert & sea—both eating at it—buried trees & houses—Rich gardens.—Pier washed by surf—like walking on reef.—Lovely situation of hotel.

Jan [1]*26 Monday.* Fine day—warm. Strolled about. Lazy heave of sea on rocks. Beautiful walk to

[1]Melville first wrote *28th* but corrected it to *26*. Again, his dates do not jibe. His last entry, before the long interlude on Jerusalem and the Missionaries, was Jan. 26th—when he broke his six days interment in Jaffa. He took a boat and rowed out to examine Jonah's pier, and returned to write of those "who have stayed in this hotel." At I P.M. of the 26th he went ashipboard, and at 2 P. M. the following day he landed at Beyrout. During the interim he must have written at sea pp. 73-99. So his 28th cannot be the 26th—especially since his earlier 26th was Saturday, and this revised 26th is Monday: unless, indeed, he was recalling the three Sundays a week in Jerusalem, and was doing his own part "to puzzle the converts."

town. Consuls[1] books. Interesting man. Luckless discussion at dinner. Young Prussian.

Jan, 27, 28, 29, 30, 31—At the hotel. Mt Leabonon—snow—sun—tropic & Pole brought into one horizon. *The gate.* Tartar couriers rushing in with tidings of war.—Quiet days—stroll out on sea shore—dash of billows—what is all this fuss about? &c—(Orientals have no hearth—no bed.—Never blush.—The Pasha's ball—The Bashi Bazouk's[2] interpretation &c—Mt Sun-Nin—River Adonis—Tranquil despondency—Burial of Janisary—Koran in palm—Party of the Pasha—interpretation of Bashi Bazouk. The Twelve Judges.[3])—Mr Wood of Concord—the Consul.

SUNDAY FEBRUARY 1ST 1857. Fine day—sea & wind abated. Paid passage (cheated) in Austrian Loyds steamer "Smirve" to Smyrna. Went on board at 3. P. M. Did not have chance to bid Mr Wood

[1]On the last page of the journal Melville records the consul's full name: George Wood of Concord, N.H.

[2]Bashi-bazouk is said to mean in Turkish: light-headed, a foolish fellow. They were irregular, ununiformed mounted troops maintained by the government; they supported themselves by robbery and extortion.

[3]The passage enclosed in parentheses is in pencil—and hence easy of erasure. I have no idea what it is all about—unless it be a cryptic sketch of the "luckless conversation at dinner" on Monday, Jan. 28th.

goodbye. Sailed at sunset. One week at Beyroot.—Very slow boat—foul bottom: poor accomodations. —Unmannerly Captain—scene at dinner table.—Captain been in America.

Feb 2d Monday. At 10. A M. sighted Cypruss. on starboard bow. Coming near long reach of whitish & yellowish coast with lofty mountains inland. From these waters rose Venus from the foam. Found it as hard to realize such a thing as to realize on Mt Olivet that from there Christ rose.—About 5. P. M. came to anchor off Larnaca the port of Cypruss. Could not well go ashore. But saw pretty much all worth seeing from deck. A level country about the town. Turkish look. Palms & minarets—houses along the shore. Export wine here. Quite a scene among the boatmen alongside. Rivalry of five boatmen for one passenger. Sunset.

Feb 3d Tuesday. Fair wind last night. At 11. A. M. came wind ahead with a very violent squall. Continued blowing for rest of day, ship horribly pitching & rolling. Seas coming from all directions.[1] Poor devils of pilgrims seasick.

Feb 4th Wednesday. Sudden change to very fine weather. The coast of Caramania in sight all day. Lofty mountains—7000 feet according to chart. Yesterday, during squall, amusing conduct of *Pan-*

[1]Known as a "confused swell."

urge[1] a Greek—thought his hour was come. Also, amusing scene in cabin at dinner. Democracy of Captain & officers. Engineer came in—sat down—drank to "the Queen!"—All Lloyds & M.J. built in England. Great source of wealth.—Beautiful evening—moonlight. Came up with Rhodes, but did not touch (though we had some Turk passengers for it) owing to the Captain's wanting to use the moonlight for getting through intricate parts of the Sporades. Rhodes looked a large & high island with some few lofty mountains inland. Recent explosion of gunpowder magazine has destroyed good part of "Street of the Chevaliers".—One finds that, after all, the most noted localities are made up of common elements of earth, air, & water.—English (Cornish) engineer invited me down to his department, and afterwards to supper in his mess. He was somewhat under stimulants. Said (pointing to his engineers)[2] "A fine pair of

[1]Rabelais, Book 4, Chapters 18-21. In the words of Panurge himself: "Nous sommes, par la vertu Dieu, troussés à ce coup. Voilà notre fanal éteint.—Zelas, zelas! Bou, bou, bou, bou. Zelas, zelas." *Consummatum est.* C'est fait de moi." Or with the addendum of Friar John: "Fi! quil est laid, le pleurard de merde."

[2]The text here is treacherous. *Engineer* is used above, and *engine* below. This word is clearly plural—and *engine* below is singular. Hence the reading, though the writing itself is ambiguous.

tools, Sir." Quite in love with his engine.—Beautiful moonlight detained me on deck late, as well as dread of my berth. Retired about 11. but at 2 A. M. was fairly goaded on deck by intolerable persecutions of bugs. Have suffered beyond telling from this cause. Not a wink of sleep now for four nights, & expect none till I get to Smyrna. This affliction of bugs & fleas & moschitos fully counterbalances to me all the satisfaction of Eastern travel.—

Thursday Feb 5th. In among the Sporades all night. Standing on t'gallant forecastle by the bright moon, Captain & officers steered us through the entanglements of channels. At dawn were completely landlocked by islands & islets. Cos, a large island, one of them. Sailed close to several. Almost jump ashore. Deep water. So thick, hard to say how you get in, or how you are to get out. All isles rocky, naked & barren. Patches of verdure on some. Fire kindled on one.—Would think this were navigation for a skiff. Passed two or three small quaint Greek vessels.—A fine sail upon the whole. But the scenery is all outline. No filling up. Seem to be sailing upon gigantic outline engravings. Shadows however help the scene. Distinct black of near isle relieved against haze of one behind. Or, terraces of bright distinctness—dusky grey—deep purple

—according to successive distances.—Serene morning. Pale blue sky.—Steered out from intricacies & saw Samos ahead, and Patmos—quite lonely looking. Patmos stands in fact quite isolated—the more so, apparently, from so suddenly coming upon it after the apple-like clusterings of the other isles. Patmos is pretty high, & peculiarly barren looking. No inhabitants.—Was here again afflicted with the great curse of modern travel—skepticism. Could no more realize that St: John had ever had revelations here, than when off Juan Fernandez, could believe in Robinson Crusoe according to De Foe.[1] When my eye rested on arid heigth, spirit partook of the barrenness.—Heartily wish Niebuhr[2] & Strauss to the dogs.—The deuce take their penetration & acumen. They have robbed us of the bloom. If they have undeceived anyone—no thanks

[1]Along right margin: ☞ The Icarian Sea, &c.

[2]This sentiment, too, gets into *Clarel*, Vol. 1, p. 136:

All now's revised:
Zion, like Rome, is Niebuhrised.
Yes, doubt attends. Doubt's heavy hand
Is set against us; and his brand
Still warreth with his natural lord—
King Common-Place—whose rule abhorred
Yearly extends in vulgar sway,
Absorbs Atlantis and Cathay;
Ay, reaches towards Diana's moon,
Affirming it a clinkered blot.

to them.—Pity that ecclesiastical countries so little attractive by nature.—Captain's story of Greek pilgrims—great part of profit of A. Lloyds from this source—Thick as cattle in pen sometimes. Save up their money for years. Like Mussulmen to Mecca.—Priests at Jerusalem sell them tickets for heaven Printed paper with Dove in middle & Father & Son each side. Divided into seats like plan of theatre on benefit night. Cant let you have *this* place—taken up. Nor *this*, but if *this* here in the corner will do—very good—may have it at 500 piastres &c.—Engineer told me about his acquaintance with Mike Walsh[1] on board this boat last year. Went to Crimea. At Trieste made speech in beer-shop to English engineers. Provoked suspicions of Austrian spy &c. Cornishman enthusiastically in love with magnanimous nature of redoubtable Mike.—He was out at elbows & borrow-

[1]See *The History of Tammany Hall*, by Gustavus Myers. Mike Walsh it was who set the classic example for the "ward-heelers" with their "gangs" that followed in his wake. Mike had an ability of a certain kind, he had a retinue of devoted "plug-ugly" followers, and those that were unmoved by his eloquence, he won over with his fists. In 1856 the Wigwam selected John Kelly to run for Congress in the district then represented by Mike Walsh—who was regarded in Washington as the leader of the rowdy element in New York City. Walsh ran independently, but Kelly beat him by 18 votes in a total vote of 7593. Then, it would appear, Mike went abroad.

ing money. The "eminentest" man in E's opinion. *Friday Feb 6th.* A cold rainy night, last night. Choice between shivering & scratching. Took both. Horrible night.—Slept awhile on settee, awoke chilled through.—Another time was all but frantic with the fleas.—The Scratching ship. Captain with back-scratcher—Two men leaning up & rubbing against each other &c. Main diversion.—In the rain entered Smyrna bay at day break. Nearly two months since here before. Hills below looked green, but mountains covered with snow.—Ashore to hotel & breakfast. Rascally waiter,—Walked in bazaar. Got bill cashed.—While at breakfast felt very bad neuralgic pain top of head—owing to utter sleeplessness of last five nights.—At 5. P. M sailed in Paddle steamer "Italia" of Lloyd's Austria Co for Pireus.—An Austrian man-of-war in harbor. Midshipmen in queer little canoes—standing up. One—alternate bender of oars.—Smoking. Honest bobtail—Stimulated. Enjoyment. Paddling in wake of steamer.—Good nights' rest. Italian merchant of Ancona.—Dried up but merry. Smoking. "Estates of the Church—Estates of de Debel!"—His ship at Constantinople Custom House.—Venetian & wife & child.—Windy boat—Temple of winds.—No comfort on deck.—Albanian taking his wine—Greek Priest.—(Little present)

Saturday Feb 7th Came to anchor at Syra—after stopping at Scio—this afternoon. Blowing hard & remained[1] through the night. Third time at Syra. Very cold to what it was before.

Feb 8th Sunday At dawn got under weigh. Head wind, head sea—cold, comfortless. Turned in to berth till four o'clock. Could not view the islands, though passing many.—Towards sunset approached Pireus.—Bare & bald aspect of the shores & isles—Came to anchor at 7. P M. Bright moonlight, with traces of the recent gales.—Men-of-war at anchor. Got into boat & ashore, & into old hack, and through a settlement like one on tow path of canal, to a McAdamed road, straight as die,—& into Athens. Passed horse & foot patrol.—Greeks in cafes smoking.—Tomorrow prepare for the Acropolis.—I saw it by moonlight from road.[2] Trying to be serious about St. John when from where I stood figure of Santon[3] a Arab holy man came between me & island — almost naked — ludicrous

[1]Unsatisfactory reading.

[2]In *Timoleon, The Apparition* (*The Parthenon uplifted on its rock first challenging the view on the approach to Athens*) (*Poems*, pp. 291-2) seems reminiscent of this moment.

[3]An indefinite article before this word would have helped the meaning. *Santon* is Spanish, derived from the Latin *sanctus*, and means "a Turkish saint." The word, as everything else, gets into *Clarel*, Vol. 1, p. 36.

chased away gravity—solemn idiocy—lunatic—opium-eater—dreamer—yet treated with profoundest respect & reverence—allowed to enter anywhere.—Wretched imbecile! base & beggarly Santon, miserable stumbling-block in way of the prophecies, since saint though though art thou art so far from inheriting the earth that thou dost not inherit a shirt to thy nakedness!

Feb 8th Sunday. After tempestuous, cold passage, came to anchor at Pireus and by moonlight to Athens. Hotel dAngleterre.[1] Alexander, guide—with Boyd who wrote Murray's G.B.—

Acropolis—blocks of marble like sticks of Wenban[2] ice—or like huge cakes of wax.—Parthenon elevated like cross of Constantine. Strange contrast of rugged rock with polished temple. At Stirling—art & nature correspond. Not so at Acropolis. Imperceptible seams—frozen together.—Bricks like cakes of snow.—

Jupiter Olympus. Like clearing in woods. clump of

[1]I have tried, by consulting guide-books of the period, to locate Melville's hotels and to estimate what he paid for his lodging. In most cases I have failed, because, it would seem, he found places that the guide-books rated as unworthy of mention. Here, however, he was situated on the Place de la Constitution, at the corner of the rue d'Hermes, and paid for pension from 17½ to 25 francs a day.

[2]The reading seems clear—but I cannot identify the ice.

columns—two isolated at further end.—Tuft of sculpture at top—Palm tree—drooping of acanthus like palm &c—Prostrate pillar in railing, like grave. Rouleau of guineas[1]—massy—base leaning—fallen pine—fell straight—still symmetric even in its fall. Stood more than 2000 years—down at last. Same night pillar of Erechtheion fell.

Feb 9th Monday. Viewed the ruins with Alexander —looked at his shop (Hymettos honey, Parnasus canes, Marathon necklaces of shell, views of Athens —dress &c.)—Mr Marshall of Boston or N.Y. at hotel. Been all over Meditteranean on ice business. Cut ice at Black Sea.—I imagined his story of life. Called on Dr King Consul. Greek wife. Invited to tea. His daughter been in America. Pleasant evening.— Cold, with intervals of snow & sun through the day.

Feb 10th Among the ruins—revisited them all.[2]

[1]One of the most baffling jobs of deciphering in the whole crabbed journal. This reading—which is certainly correct— was achieved by Miss Dorothy Brewster.

[2]In *Timoleon,* in the section *Fruit of Travel Long Ago,* there are two poems on *The Attic Landscape,* a poem in four parts on *The Parthenon,* poems on *Greek Masonry, Greek Architecture, The Archipelago, Disinterment of Hermes,* and *The Apparition* (just above referred to). The impression of Athens upon him was patently profound. In his early manhood he had fled from New England to Polynesia; and the more immediate contrast between the Holy Land and Hellas made him feel

"The All-in-All seems here a Greek."

Temple of Theseus well preserved. Yellowish look—saffron—burnt in slow fire of Time. *Temple of Victory*—resurrection—figure of Victory tying her sandal—grace & loveliness of the whole conception.—Genoese tower incorporating columns of Peristyle.—Pavement of Parthenon—square—blocks of ice frozen together.—No mortar:—Delicacy of frost-work.

Spent evening conversing with young English officer from Cephalonia—Told story of Lindy Foote's son.[1] &c.—Saw the sunset from LYCCABETUS. Lovely climb.

Feb 11th Wednesday. Clear & beautiful day. Fine ride on box to Piraeus. Acropolis in sight nearly whole way. Straight road. Fully relieved against the sky—Between Hymettos & Pentelicos. Pentelicos covered at top with snow—looking down on its child, the Parthenon:—Ruins of Parthenon like North River breaking up. &c—At two P. M embarked in French steamer "Cydnus" for Messina. Noble vessel & French-built. Two or three Englishmen on board—young men—talk with them. Misseri[2]

[1]Lindy Foote eludes every research I have made for him—or her. Lindy Foote is probably an obvious, and doubtlessly an interesting person.

[2]By Kinglake spelled *Mysseri.*

(Eōthen's)[1] on board, going to England. Talk with him.—Sailed along coast of Morea—mountainous. Good bed & slept well.

Feb 12th Thursday. Head wind & not fair overhead. but fast steamer. Quite a number in Second Cabin. No land in sight today.

Feb 13th Friday. Coasts of Calabria & Sicily ahead at day break. Neared them at 10 o'clock. Both very high & broken—picturesque. Many houses. Snow

[1]*Eōthen:* both the name of a book, and the nick-name of its author, Alexander William Kinglake (1809-1891). " 'Eōthen' is, I hope" so says Kinglake in a note in his Preface, "almost the only hard word to be found in the book; it is written in Greek ἠῶθεν,— (Atticè with an aspirated ε instead of the η)—and signifies, 'from the early dawn',—'from the East'—*Donn Lex., 4th edition.*" Kinglake had gone into Asia Minor "when Lalla Rookh was young" and returned to write an anonymous account of his journeying subtitled: *Traces of Travel Brought Home from the East.* "My excuse for the book is its truth," Kinglake wrote. "My narrative is not merely righteously exact in matters of fact (where fact is in question), but it is true in this larger sense—it conveys—not those impressions which *ought to have been* produced upon any 'well constituted mind', but those which were really and truly received at the time of his rambles, by a headstrong, and not very amiable traveller, whose prejudices in favor of other people's notions were then exceedingly slight. As I have felt, so I have written." And this is really the precisely same temper in which Melville had in *Typee* told of Polynesia. It is an unorthodox and particularly brilliant work, frequently paralleling Melville's own impressions of God's Own Country when he got to it; as when at Jerusalem Kinglake found the

on tops of highest mountains. Fine sail in the Straits. At 1 P. M. anchored in harbor of Messina. Fine harbor. Like lagoon. Rainy day. Landed at Police. Searched for papers &c. Hotel in noble street. Large church. Coat cleaned.

Feb 14th Saturday. Last night went to Cafe near opera-house to meet, if I might, Dr Lockwood of the frigate. But did not. This morning pleasant weather. Many American vessels in port for fruit.

Holy Sepulchre vulgarized into a Bartholomew Fair where they "transact salvation." I owe among my many debts to Melville, and not among the least, his initiating me into Kinglake.

Eōthen appeared in 1844; *Typee*, two years later. They are books very similar in appeal. And it is pleasant to know that as two young men-of-letters, Kinglake and Melville met even for a moment in the flesh. In the journal of his visit to London in 1849, under the date of Sunday, Dec. 23, Melville wrote: "This morning breakfasted with Mr. Rogers again, and there met "Barry Cornwall," otherwise Mr. Proctor, and his wife —and Mr. Kinglake (author of *Eōthen*). A very pleasant morning we had, and I went away at quarter past one o'clock." But it is more remarkable that eight years later Melville should have rubbed shoulders with Mysseri—if he really did; for it is a too perfect realization of André Gide's ideal of fiction, to be compatible with history. "The accomplished Mysseri"—to quote *Eōthen*—"of whom you have heard me speak so often, and who served me so faithfully throughout my oriental journeys, acted as our interpreter, and was, in fact, the brain of our corps." In *Eōthen* he is most engagingly portrayed. There is an illuminating life of Kinglake by W. Tuckwell (London, 1902). In this biography, unfortunately, Melville is not mentioned.

This the season. Went on board one. Went off to friggate. Called on Cap. Bell. Saw Dr Lockwood. Went with him on donkeys to a high hill four miles distant. The telegraph. Dined with him & officers in ward-room of friggate. Passed off pleasantly. Then walked through the town with the Dr, and in evening went to the opera of Macbeth with him. Retired at 11 P. M.—The officers of U.S.F. Constellation are

Captain Bell	Lieut Fauntleroy (Virginian)
1st Lieut Porter	Mid. Buchanan.
2d " Bankhead	Cap. Clerk. Bell.
— " Spicer	

The forts of Messina command the town, not the sea. Large tract of town demolished, so as to have rest at command from fort. Dial in church. Streams from mountains coming through the town.

Feb 15th Sunday. Dr Lockwood called at hotel, sat, and then proposed long walk. Walked out in lovely suburbs skirting the sea. Calabria's mountains in sight. Salvator Rosa look of them. Met masques on the road. Carnival. Walked 7 or 8 miles. Sat on stones, much talk. Fine day. Enjoyed it considerably. Back to dinner at hotel by 6 P. M. Streets very lively in evening. Walked about with Dr. till 10 o'clock. Cafe—habitue's.

Monday & Tuesday, 16 & 17 Feb. Neapolitan steamer for Naples started at 1 P. M today. Took 2d cabin passage. Repented it sorely in the end. Crossed the Straits to Reggio (St. Paul) lay there till midnight. By day break stopped at another place, high on hill, (Murat shot)[1] and at noon at a third place on coast. Fine weather. Calm & beautiful. Populous shores & very mountainous & high. Scenery very fine. Sailed close in shore. Suffered again horribly from sleeplessness. (Saw Etna from Reggio) *Wed. 18 Feb.* Ere day break we passed between Capri & main & entered bay of Naples. I was on deck. Dim mass of Vesuvius soon in sight. Recognized it from pictures of mother's. Soon, *smelt* the city. Brilliant lights.—Detained on board till 9 A. M. by Police being dilatory. Went to *Hotel de Geneve* with some others. Struck by first appearance of Naples. Great crowds, noble streets, lofty houses. —At breakfast Rhinelander & Friedman said they were going to Pompeii. Joined them. R.R. same thing over the world. Passed through Portici, Resina, Torre del Greco.—Pompeii like any other town. Same old humanity. All the same whether one be dead or alive. Pompeii comfortable sermon. Like Pompeii better than Paris,[2]—Guards there.

[1]Below the small town of Pizzo, situated on a rock, are the ruins of an old castle where Joachim Murat, king of Naples, was shot on the thirteenth of October, 1815.

[2]Melville was once in Paris: between November 28 and December 6, 1849.

Silent as Dead Sea.—To Vesuvius on horse back. Vineyards about the base. Ashy climb. Hanging on to guide. Haggling. Old crater of Pompeii. Modern crater like old abandoned quarry—burning . . . . .[1] —Red & yellow. Bellowing. Bellows. flare of flame. Went into crater. Frozen liquorice.—Came down with a rush. Dusk. Ride in dark. At Nunziata[2] got veturino to Naples. Cold ride, no coat,—back to hotel by midnight. Silent country & streets. One suburb. Ate & to bed.

Thursday Feb 19th. Sallied out for walk by myself. Strada de Toledo.[3] Noble street. Broadway. Vast crowds. Splendor of city. Palace—soldiers—music —clang of arms all over city. Burst of troops from archway.[4] Cannon posted inwards. Royal carriages in palace—royal steamer. To Capo di Monte in cab. Superb palace, roads, grounds, & view. St. Januarius of the Poor. Catacombs—old man with lanthorn. Great extent. Old times. Grimy. Couldn't get away. Thought crazy.—Walked about again. Bought good coat for $9.—Quays show little commerce. Wonder how live here. Magnificence of the city. Vesuvius in sight from square. Smoking.—

[1]Undecipherable.

[2]Torre dell'Annunziata.

[3]The Via Roma.

[4]Amplified by Melville in the second section of *Naples in the Time of Bomba* (*Poems*, 380 ff.).

Walked to Villa Real—hotels—at Brittanique happened to see Townsend's name.—Dined there. Relieved by hearing (tho' but indirectly) from home. To San Carlo at 10 o'clock. Fine house. Met English banker. Sentinel on stage. &c.

Friday Feb 20th. Walked to Post Office with letters. Then took voiture for Eastern part of bay. Posilipo —beautiful promontory of villas—along the sea— new road—till came in sight of Pozzuoli. Went through Grotto of Sejanus to remains of School of Virgil & other ruins of villas. Ruined stone balcony overhanging deep cave & cliff. Isle of Nisida. Saw Baia—the end of the bay. Went to the Solfatara—smoke—landscape not so very beautiful.— Sulphurous & aridity, the end of the walk. (At Posilipo found not the cessation which the name expresses.)[1] Passed lake of Agano (salt at bottom) (Avernus did not visit—much the same, I suppose) Visited Grotto del Cane. Old man leading poor patient little dog. Unlocked gate.—Dog keeled over, gasped, insensible. Dragged out & came to— lay on grass, roled & walked patiently off.—Poor victim.—Returned to Naples by Grotto of Posilipo.

[1]παυσίλυπος, meaning "ending pain." In *Pausilippo (In the Time of Bomba)* (*Poems*, pp. 280-2) Melville elaborates this.

Its name, in pristine years conferred
By settling Greeks, imports that none
Who take the prospect thence can pine.

Very high. Scene of thoroughfare in Grotto. Smacking of whips, goats, twilight,—Sun streams through at sunset.—Villa Real—splendid equipages. Visited Virgil's tomb—mere ruin—high up. Great view of bay & Naples & Vomero Mount & Castle of Elmo. Drove up to Elmo Castle. Long street. From balcony over garden of Church of San Martino got glorious view of bay & town. Sunset. White friars.—Drove to Cafe de la Europe for cheap dinner. Row with cabman. Dined & walked for a hour in Strada de Toledo. Great crowds. Could hardly tell it from Broadway. Thought I was there.—Cafes well filled.—Many lottery shops, all with little shrine of Virgin & child, lit—cheap decoration. Curious reflections. Religious inducement to wickedness.—Home by 9 & to bed.

Saturday 21st Feb. Upon going from chamber in morning encountered by jabbering man with document. Commissioner. Into breakfast room—people at table—"Do any of you speak French?" Whereupon Mr Rouse (?)[1] spoke. Passport. &c.—Went to Rothschild's for £20. No scrutiny as at other places. Went to Museum. A collection of them. *Bronze utensils from Pompeii & Herculaneum.*—

[1]Melville questions his own spelling; he seems never to have quite made up his mind as to the correct spelling of this name.

Helmet & skull.—Dentist tools—Surgical tools—furnaces—mosaic tables & pavements—fishhooks—mirrors for toilette—cash cabinets.

Terra cotta collection—mythological delineations.

Hall of bronze statuary.[1] Plato (hair & beard & imperial) Nero (villianous) Seneca (caricature.) Drunken faun on wine skin. Augustus. horse—colossal head of horse—&c&c.

Paintings Madonna by Raphael—a Domenichino. Two small Corregios—(could not see anything so wonderful in these last) But face of Raphael's Madonna touchingly maternal. A vast collection of other pictures I but glanced at.

Frescoes—from Diomed's house—fruit pieces &c from dining room.

Marbles. Hercules Farnese—colossal. gravely benevolent face. The group of the bull; glorious.—Tomb

[1]Between 1857 and 1861, Melville went on the lecture platform. He spoke on two topics: *The South Seas*, and *Statuary in Rome*. On December 2, 1857, in Boston, Melville lectured on the latter of his topics. The lecture was reported in the Boston *Journal* the following day. "The speaker then vividly described the statues of Senece, with the visage of a pawn broker; Nero, the fast young man; Plato with the locks and air of an exquisite, as if meditating on the destinies of the world under the hand of a hair-dresser. Thus these statues confess, and, as it were, prattle to us of much that does not appear in history and the written works of those they represent."

stones &c with inscriptions, identical with ours.—
—Had to quit Museum ere through with it.
Went in voiture to Cathedral of St. Januarius. Very fine. Thence a promiscuous drive through the older & less elegant part of town. Long narrow lanes. Arches, crowds.—
Tumblers in narrow street.[1] Blocked way. Balconies with women. Cloth on ground. They gave way, after natural reluctance. Merriment. Turned round & gave the most grateful & graceful bow I could. Handkerchiefs waved from balconies, good humored cries &c—Felt prouder than an Emperor. Shabby old hack, but good fellow, driver.—Wonderful number of shops &c. Crowds of idlers. Lazzaroni troublesome. Stopped in at curious little old chapel. Statue in net.—Dismissed hack at hotel.—Walked on mole.—Military continually about streets.—Curious bells near my room. Every ten minutes strike. Repeat each other. Conversation of bells. Tete-a-tete.—Dined at hotel de Geneve at 5 P. M.—Uncertain about diligence or vetturino to Rome. Paid a Napoleon for getting passport in order.
Sunday 22d Feb. Breakfasted early and at 9 o'clock took train for Castleamare[2] (In the corner) with

[1]This incident is recounted with heavy elaboration in *Naples in the Time of Bomba* (*Poems*, pp. 378-380).
[2]Castellamare.

Mr Rows of Brunswick (N.J) and young Englishman.—Volcanic formation along road. Crowds of hackmen &c. Vetturinos bargaining. Three hours, with coach berths, at least. To Sorrento for about a dollar.—Grand drive. Road. Windings broad sweeps & curves—ravines—bridge—terrace—rocks —inclined plain—heigth—sea—Sorrento. Tasso's house, hotel. Beauty of site on cliff overhanging sea —c. Disappointment about vetturino. Some mystery of general procedure.—Got man to speak English & engaged 1st seat in coupe for 24th Feb.—Mr R. a little queer at dinner. His sister affable. *Monday 23d Feb.* Went to Museum after breakfast. Shut. Took hack and went on Pausilipo road. Fine morning. Repassed the scenery of the other day as far as hill (semi circular turnout) whence you get view of bay of Pozzuoli. Drove to village of that name. Thence to Lake Avernus. In a crater Lonely look. Flags on water side. Melancholy old temple. Curious they should have fabled hell here. Cave of Sybil. Gate. (Narrow one to hell, here) Torches. Long grotto, many hundred feet, fast walk. Came to sudden dive down—very narrow—Descent to Infernal regions, guide said—Came to pool—took me on his shoulder across—bath & bed of Sybil—oracle—place—Landed me on ledge of rock.—Many other caves to right & left. Infernal enough.

—What in God's name were such places made for, & why? Surely man is a strange animal. Diving into the bowels of the earth rather than building up towards the sky. How clear an indication that he sought darkness rather than light.—Before coming to Lucrino (near the sea, divided by causeway; very stagnant & bad smell—"hotel" overlooking it) you see the New Mountain. Curious to see this strange (parvenue) from the abyss taking his rank among the elderly mountains. But not so *new*, either. Could tell queer stories. "But that the secrets of his prison-house &c"
Comparison between Avernus & Hinnom.[1]
New Mountain cultivated towards summit. Buildings on it.—Pozzuoli a great bay in bay. Drive to Baie. Along the shore. Road cut through ruins of old villas of Romans. Singular melting together of art in ruins and Nature in vigor. Vines overrunning ruins. Ruins here take the place of rocks. Arches, substructures, buttresses &c &c &c.
Temple of Venus. Round. Summit wavy with verdure—corpses dressed for a ball. Temple of Mercury. Low dome. Part fallen & below. Vines

[1]A valley outside of Jerusalem, notorious for the rites of Baal. "And they have built the high places of Tophet, which is in the valley of the son of Hinnom, to burn their sons and daughters in the fire"—Jeremiah, 7, 31.

drooping down. Echo. Where art thou, Mercury—Where?

On the western shore of Italy is a bay &c—A burning mountain—enumerate the monstrousness of the remorselessness of Nature—ravages of war &c—burned city. Solfatara &c.—Now, one would think if any *modern* city were here built &c, they would be sober in view of these things. But no. Gayest city in the world. No equipages flash like these; no beauties so haughty. No cavaliers so proud, no palaces so sumptuous, &c &c.—Apt representation of that heedlessness, benignly ordained, of man which prevents one generation from learning from a past.—"Let us eat, drink & be merry, for tomorrow we die". Such seems the lesson learned by the Neopolitans from their scenery.—The beauty of the place in connection with its perilousness. — Skaters on ice. — [Full, too, of monuments of the variety of old religions (Sybils cave) and yet the Romish superstition.

═══════ Arrived at hotel at 4 P. M. & prepared to pack valise to leave at Diligence office overnight, after writing this scrawl of memoranda . . . .
Next for

ROME.[1]

[1]Behind the exaggerated flourish with which Melville announces his next destination was undoubtedly a long-

P.S.

Wonderful old ruins palace at Pausilippo. Sea-palace.—The road. Villas, grottoes, summer-houses—ravines—bowers &c &c &c.

Such a profusion & intricacy of grotto, grove, gorge villa hill, that it takes some time & patience to disentangle such snarls of beauty.—Of the ride to Pausillippo.—

Scene at dinner table tonight. Comments &c. The young Parisian, the fair young lady, the French judge with black cap on. (Sentencing cap)[1]

Tuesday Feb 24th At 8 A. M. started in diligence from P.O in Naples for Rome. (☞ For Rome see page at end of book)[2] Only Frenchman & self in coupe. Like balcony overlooking houses. Snug. Far preferable to steamer &c.—Fine level country about Naples. Vines abundant. Smart postillion—one continual gallop & crack of the whip from post to post. Change horses 8 miles. At least 100 horses at this diligence. At Fondi passed our veturino friend. Saw various ruins from time to time. At night fall

cherished wish to see the Holy City. In his 1849 Journal, on November 17, after he had failed to make as advantageous arrangement with publishers as he had hoped, he wrote: "Bad news enough—I shall not see Rome—I'm floored—Appetite unimpaired however—"

[1]In pencil.

[2]In pencil, along right margin.

entered among mountains. The tower & sea at Terracina. Night.

Wednesday Feb 25th At daybreak were on the Alban mount. At 10 A. M were in Rome. First letter from home. Stopped at hotel de Minerva.[1] In square is obelisk on elephant.[2] Walked to Capital. Took view from tower. Whether it is having coming from the East, or chafed mood, or what, but Rome fell flat on me. Oppressively flat.—Didn't sleep any last night, though.—Tiber a ditch, yellow as saffron. The whole landscape nothing independent of associations. St: Peters looks small from Tower of Capital.—Walked to St. Peters. Front view disappointing. But grand approach. Interior comes up to expectations. But dome not so wonderful as St: Sophia's.—Exhausted at 3. P M. Dined at 6 & to bed.

Thursday Feb 26.—To Tortoni's, banker, to find out about S. Shaw or letters.[3] Learnt nothing. To Capital & Coliseum.—Coliseum like great hollow

[1]Centrally situated, and still flourishing.

[2]Melville first wrote *hippopotamus*.

[3]Samuel Shaw (1833-1915) was Melville's younger brother-in-law. At this time he had been travelling on the continent and getting occasional bulletins of Melville. In a letter written him on Christmas by his mother, and addressed to him in Germany, a post-script says: "Elizabeth has not had one word from Herman since her husband left Liverpool for

among hills. Hopper of Greylock.[1] Slope of concentric ruins overgrown. Mountainous. Museum of Capital. Hall of Emperors. "That Tiberius? he dont look so bad at all"—It was he. A look of sickly evil,—intellect without manliness & sadness without goodness. Great brain overrefinements. Solitude.—Dying Gladiator. Shows that humanity existed among the barberousness of the Roman time, as it now among Christian barberousness. Antinous, beautiful.—Walked to the Pincian hill—gardens & statuary.—overlooking Piazza del Popolo.—Fashion & Rank—Preposterous touring within stone's throw of Antinous. How little influence has truth in the world!—Fashion everywhere ridiculous, but most so in Rome. (Music on Pincian). No place where lonely man will feel more lonely than in Rome. (or Jerusalem). Fine view of St Peters from Pincian.—In the evening walked to Cafe Greco, in Via Condotti. "English sculptor" with dirty hands &c. Dense smoke. Rowdy looking chaps. &c—Home & to bed. (Stopped at evening

Constantinople." And Samuel's brother Lemuel, addressing him (still in Germany) on January 11, concludes with an almost verbatim repetition of his mother's complaint, and adds: "I don't know how or where you are to look for him & know no way of communication with him except through Bentley of London." Both of these letters are unpublished.

[1]See the dedication of *Pierre*.

in picture dealers; offered a Cenci for $4. Surprisingly cheap). Fine lounge in Piazza di Espagna among picture & curiosity dealers, & in Via Condotti, also.

Friday Feb 27th Tried to find A. Consul, Page, & Jarves.[1] Failed in all.—Went to Baths of Caracalla. —Wonderful. Massive. Ruins form, as it were, natural bridges of tousands of arches. There are glades, & thickets among the ruins—high up.— Thought of Shelley. Truly, he got his inspiration here. Corresponds with his drama & mind. Still majesty, & desolate grandeur.—After much trouble & sore travel without a guide managed to get to Protestant Burial Ground & pyramid of Cestius under walls. Read Keats' epitaph. Separated from

[1]A. Consul I take to be not a proper name, but merely the American Consul. Page appears later, as does a note on him. It is a pity Melville did not succeed in finding James Jackson Jarves (1818-1888), who, in 1840, had published the first newspaper to appear in Honolulu. It is possible that in the South Seas he and Melville may have met. Melville arrived in Honolulu in the early part of 1843, where, according to Arthur Stedman, he was "employed as a clerk"; though he appears to have been in Honolulu only four months (see Appendix to *Typee*). In any event, Jarves' enthusiasms swung from Polynesia to Italy, and in 1850 he settled in Florence as a pioneer art collector and voluminous writer. As is usual with the persons mentioned by Melville in this journal, he was an exceptionally picturesque character.

the adjacent ground by trench.—Shelley in other ground. Plain stone.—(Went from Caracalla to Shelley's grave by natural process) Thence to Cenci Palace, by way of Suspension Bridge, Isle of Tiber, theatre of Marcellus (blacksmith shop &c in arches—black with centuries (of) grime & soot —built upon above & inhabited)—Orsini Palace & Ghetto. Tragic looking place enough. The big sloping arch.—Part of it inhabited, part desolate. —Thence to Farnese palace—finest architecture of all the palaces (prints). Farnese Hercules & Farnese Toro formerly here. Now in Museum Borbanuco,[1] Naples. Thence to St. Angelo Bridge & St. Peters. And to dinner & bed.—Remarked[2] the banks of Tiber near St: Angelo—fresh, alluvial look near masonry—primeval as Ohio in the midst of all these monuments of the centuries.

Saturday Feb 28th Lost time going after Consul &c. At 12 M. was at Borghese villa. Extent of grounds—peculiar odor of Italian gardens—deep groves—cold splendor of villa—Venus & Cupid—mischievous look of C.—Thence to Villa Albani—along the walls—Antinous—head like moss-rose with curls & buds—rest all simplicity—end of fillet on shoulder —drapery, shoulder in the mantle—hand full of

[1]The National Museum.

[2]Questionable reading.

flowers & eyeing them—the profile &c. The small bronze Apollo. Surprising how such a metal could be melted into such flexible-looking forms. Picture of Italian lady.—Thence to the Gate Pia to fountain of Moses. not bad—Ox drinking—pitchers &c crowded round.—Thence to baths of Diocletian—Church—monument of 8 columns.—S. Rosa's tomb. The four fountains—Monte Cavallo—colossal horses from ruins of baths—like finding the bones of the mastadon—gigantic figures emblematic of gigantic Rome. Hill of Monte Cavallo. View of dome of St. Peters.—Thence by Trajan's forum home at 6 P. M. dinner & to bed.—Extent of ground not built upon within walls of Rome. Silence & loneliness of long streets of blank garden walls.

Sunday March 1st 1857. To Monte Cavallo—colossal equestrian group, found in Baths, basin also, obelisk—most imposing group of antiques in Rome. —People these Caracalla baths anew with these colossal figures—Gigantic Rome.—St. Peters in its magnitude & colossal statuary seems an imitation of these fragments.—The grass growing in the Square. The 4 Fountains. 4 Vistas—terminating with obelisks &c.—the . . . . . .[1] old palaces—The ruinous fountain of rocks, the vines &c trailing into pool. The mossy pillars & green ooze of loneliness.

[1]Illegible.

—The poor old statues in their niches—the gardens. —Santa Maria Maggiore.—(The picture at home) Gold from Peru.—Trophies of Marius & several other ruins. The Porta Maggore. Finest ancient gate in Rome. Baker's Tomb.[1] Acqueduct—mass of brick.—To the basilica of St: John Lateran. Loneliness of the spot by Giovanni Gate (Naples) height looking down from wall,—Splendor of private tombs there. 12 Apostles gigantic—drapery.—Did not visit stairs &c—Walk along the walls outside.—Solitude & silence—passing gates walled up —passing the gate Totilla entered—perfect hush of all things—The gardens outside—To the gate of St: Sebastian—ancient. Arch of Drusus—Columbaria—Dove-cote—The little busts. Darby & Joan, hand in hand—domestic expressions—man the same—. Scipio's tomb. Extent of it—inscriptions—candles.—Notification over gate—Penny-Fair.—Palace of the Caesars—Went in—Great arch over arch — stairs — birds — stables. — Arch of Janus. —Cloaca Maxima—gloomy hole—trailing ruins into the sewer.—Lost my way getting back. Stopped in at church. Animated preacher. Home by 5 P. M. Dinner & to bed.

[1]In the form of an oven, and in its way a prototype for Trimalchio. Erected by the baker Marcus Vergilius Eurysaces himself during his lifetime.

March 2d 1857. Vatican Day (Monday) from 12 to 3 in Museum; previously visiting the Loggie of Raphael & Sistine Chapel. The Loggie—piazza—sky seen between columns—Adam & Eve—The Eve—Faded bloom of the paintings.—Staid in Vatican till closed. Fagged out completely, & sat long time by the obelisk, recovering from the stunning effect of a first visit to the Vatican.—Went to Piazza de Espagna, & home.—Sat a while in the Rowes' room ere retiring.—Hall of Animals[1]—Wolf & sheep.[2]

March 3d Tuesday. Started with Mr & Mrs R. to ascend St. Peters. Too late for time.—Visited Mosaic Museum in Vatican. Heads of Popes from St. Paul. Rode to Palazza Barberini to see Cenci. —Expression of suffering about the mouth—(appealing look of innocence) not caught in any copy or engraving.[3]—Lovely little painting of Galatea

[1]A room in the Vatican containing a number of animal pieces.

[2]Is Melville intending a pronouncement upon his host? Earlier he had written in Naples: "Mr. R. a little queer at dinner. His sister affable."

[3]There can be no doubt that the Cenci exerted upon Melville an almost obsessional fascination; first he goes shopping for a Cenci print, then to the Cenci palace (after thoughts of Shelley), and then to the Barberini Palace to see the painting. See *Pierre*, and in especial the last two wild books with the incestuous dream and "that sweetest, most

in car—Two swimmers in dark blue shadowed water—gleam of limbs.—A Holbein (Christ disputing with doctors) To San Maria Maggiore. To St. John Lateran—Corsini Chapel—gems in crown —statue below in vault—"ThePieta"—Scala Santa —(5 stairs) pilgrims going up—penitents.— Walked to Trevi Fountain.—Very fine.—A cold rain, windy, dirty & horribly disagreeable day. Dinner & to bed.—The Peruvian & Pole.—The Irish priest. *March 4th Wednesday.* Ascended St. Peters. feilds & paddocks on top—figures of saints.—Met Mr & Mrs C. & brother on the church.—To Corsini Palace —paintings—large gallery—& very many first rate works. Holbein's Luther & wife—Magdalen of Carlo Dolci.—Battle scene of Salvator Rosa & one Calabrian scene. To church of St. Pietro in Mon-

touching, but most awful of all feminine heads—The Cenci of Guido." And *Clarel* (Vol. 2, p. 33):

He wore that nameless look
About the mouth—so hard to brook—
Which in the Cenci portrait shows,
Lost in each copy, oil or print;
Lost, or else slurred, as 'twere a hint
Which if received, few might sustain:
A trembling over of small throes
In weak swoll'n lips, which to restrain
Desire is none, nor any rein.

This appears in a context as baffling and as amazing as anything in *Pierre*.

torio—Flagellation of Piombo[1]—View of Rome. To the Fountain Paolino—largest in city. Another noble view.—Crossed the Janiculum Bridge to Saint Andrea della Valle—Frescoed cupola—Early to bed.

March 5th Thursday. To Coliseum. To Villa built upon arches of palace of Caesars. To Capitol. Through gallery a second time. Bronze wolf. To Borgese Gallery. Drive. C. Borgia. To Pincian Hill. Cold grey windy day. Eye so bad had to go to room & to bed at 5 P. M. minus dinner.[2]

March 6th Friday. Eye prevented me from doing or seeing much today. To St. Peters—Borghese Gallery—Pincian—Saw the Pope[3] in carriage—Funeral of French officer—lane among high walls covered with green foliage—Talk with Mr R. in his room.

March 7th Saturday. To Sciarra Gallery. Faded splendor—balcony over Corso—closeness of a closet—The Cheating Gamblers (Honesty & Knavery—the self-possession & confidence of knavery—the

[1]The painter, and not the victim.

[2]As early as 1850 we have evidence of Melville's suffering from his eyes. Then he wrote: "My evenings I spend in a sort of mesmeric state in my room—not being able to read—" or "my writing won't be very legible, because I am keeping one eye shut and wink at the paper with the other." See Meade Minnigerode's *Some Personal Letters of Herman Melville*, 69 ff; and *Pierre*, Book XXV, Chapter III.

[3]Pius IX.

irresolution & perplexity of honesty)—The Gloaming (to apply a Scotch word) of a scene between dusk & dark of Claude. Other Claudes (His first manner) All their effect is of atmosphere. He paints the air. Curious Holy Family of Albert Durer (the old nurse) A Lady by Titian—The crimson & white sleeves—The golden haze of his pictures (Danae) The Sciarra have been in Chancery.—*To the Rospigliosi Gallery*—The terraced garden—200 years old—the garden stairway in hollow—massy balustrades—The lemon walk tiled over—The fish pond & fountains & violets wet with spray—The Casino—bas-reliefs—Aurora[1]—Floats overhead like sun-dyed clouds—The Mirror[2]—the lovers seated there. Samson pulling down the temple[3]—gigantic—unfortunate hint at fall of Aurora—The shot.—*To the Quirinale Palace of Pope.* Vast hall—cold splendor—Marbles, paintings, &c&c&c Gobelins—The palm—Sevres china—Guido's Annunciation (Raphael's) Fresco of the Swiss Guards looking down—boxes with ribands—*The Gardens*—A Paradise without the joy—freaks & caprices of endless wealth—rheumatics in gardener—As stone

[1]The ceiling painting, by Guido Reni.

[2]Placed opposite the entrance for the convenience of viewing the ceiling.

[3]On the entrance wall.

is sculptured into forms of foliage, so here foliage trained into forms of sculpture—walls, niches, arches, casements, columns, bases, chambers (quarried out of foliage)—The arcades—leafy cloisters—The water-organ—the Vulcan's shop—the fountains.—*To Church out of Bath*—Monumental columns—Greek Cross.—To little gem of church in street leading to Porta Pia—The gems—the cherubs looking down from cupola—the precious marbles. —Dined on 19 cents at Lepri's in Via Condotti & home & to bed. Eye very troublesome. Hope it wont stay so.

March 8th Sunday To Jesuits Church—To Gibbon's Church[1] nigh Capitol—various columns rifled from ancient edifices—Gibbon's meditations[2]—Christianity.—To Baths of Titus—overgrown—dark & intricate—resort of banditti once.—To Mamertine Prison—To Tarpeian—dirty yard at base—Dignified Roman guide—"*Miserable!*"—Pitiable object.—To St Peters—tour of interior—

[1]Santa Maria in Aracoeli. According to mediaeval tradition it occupies the site where the Tiburtine Sibyl foretold the imminent coming of Christ.

[2]"It was at Rome, on the 15th of October, 1764, as I sat musing amidst the ruins of the Capital while the barefooted Friars were singing vespers in the temple of Jupiter, that the idea of writing the decline and fall of the city first started in my mind."

Stuarts' tomb.[1] The Popes m . . . . s.[2] To Pincian —great Sunday resort.—Dined on 17 cents & to bed at 11 P M after a talk with Mr R. in his room.

March 9th Monday. Vatican day.—Deliberate walk through the galleries.—Hall of Animals—Wolf & lamb, paw uplifted, tongue—fleece. Dog on stag, eying him. Lion on horse.—But Playing Goats—the goat & kid —show a Wordsworthian appreciation of the gentle in Nature.—Frescoed ceilings, which, like starry skies, no man regards—so plentiful are the splendors.— Coronation of the Virgin—Raphael—The faces so like his masters Perugino's in the next room.— Review of troops in St Peters piazza.—With Mr & Miss Rouse to St. Onofrio, church & monastery, where Tasso expired. On the Janiculum, fine view of Rome. Sad corridors, cloisters & no grass. Doleful old chamber—wax casts.—Little sad garden, moulding gateways.—Quaint church—damp & doleful. —New monument in wretched taste.—Stopped in at some churches & to Lepri, to soup & meat.

March 10th Tuesday. I begin writing here after more than one week's abstinence, owing to state of my eyes and general incapacity. On the day of this date I went to the Doria Pamfili palace in the

[1]In the chapel next the Baptistery are monuments of the wife of the Old Pretender and the last Stuarts.

[2]Except for the first and last letters, undecipherable.

morning. Most elegant one in Rome perhaps. Two portraits of Raphael. One of Titian's women—profuse brown hair on Magdalen—Thought I detected a resemblance between it & his portrait of his wife —only the Magdalen idealized. Machiavelli's portrait disappointed me. Ugly profile, &c. Did'nt like it. Two large landscapes of Claude did not touch me. The "Gloaming" is the best. Brueghel's pictures much pleased me. The Elements & animals.—Lucretia Borgia—no wicked look about her. Good looking dame—rather fleshy.—To the Borghese Gallery for the third time.—The serpent table there—the tunnel cut thro' to street, & fountain. Have remarked before on pictures here.—To the studios.[1] The English sculptor, Gibson.[2] His colored Venus. Talk with him. The 7 branched candlestick &c. Art perfect among Greeks.[3] Limit to human power, –perfection.—To Bartholomew's.[4]

[1]See Henry James' *William Wetmore Story and His Friends* (2 vols. Boston, 1903).

[2]John Gibson (1790-1866) was the first Englishman to color his statues—first as a mere border to the drapery of a portrait statue of Victoria, and by degrees extending it to the entire flesh, as in his "tinted Venus."

[3]Who of course tinted their statuary.

[4]Edward Bartholomew (1822-1858) started as a dentist's assistant. He took to painting, and in time discovered that he was color-blind. Small-pox was followed by a hip affliction that crippled him. He migrated to Italy as a sculptor.

His Eve. Bust of young Augustus—(Edition).[1] To Page's.[2] Thin socks. Titian[3]—kneading of flesh—Middle tint. Long lecture.—Home, dinner, bed.

March 11th Wednesday. Started for Appian Way. Narrow,—not like Milton's Way—not suitable to dignity &c. Old pavement. Tomb with olive trees on it. Sown in corruption, raised in olives.[4] Same day, Grotto of Egeria. Nothing very beautiful or at all striking about it. No foliage, but one clump. —To St. Pauls, outside walls. Magnificent. Malaria among the gilding. Building against Nature. Pet of Pio's. The Catacombs—labyrinth of them.—Home at 3, changed room, had fire, and prepared for being laid up. No dinner.

Thursday March 12th. Crept out at 12 M. to Coliseum. Repeopling it, &c. The arch. Dined on fig & bread.

[1]The reading is both doubtful, and, so far as I can discover, meaningless.

[2]William Page (1811-1885). Though at the age of eleven he took a prize at the American Institute for a pen-and-ink drawing, he was in a law office for a while, spent two years as a student of divinity, painted under Morse, migrated to Italy in 1849, patented various improvements in guns and boats, experimented in all sorts of mediums and methods in painting greatly to the detriment of his pictures, and died a Swedenborgian. For a time he was a neighbor of Elihu Vedder, another Swedenborgian, to whom Melville dedicated *Timoleon.*

[3]Page's admiration for Titian was unbounded.

[4]One of Melville's favorite witticisms.

Friday March 13th. Fine day. To grounds of Villa Borghese. Great beauty of them. Fine rich odors of bushes & trees. The laurel &c. The closed villa, statues seen thro' railing. Silence & enchantment. "Glitter wide the halls, high the laurel groves &c. —Taken from scenery of Italia's Villa.—Called on Page. Long lecture. Swedenburgh. Spiritualist. Thin socks.[1] Dined on a plate at Lepri's.

Saturday March 14th. Walked about to Trinita di Monte. Second went to Albani Villa. Father Murphy. Mrs. S. Caryatide. The long lines of foliage—architecture of villa, richness of landscape. Fine site. —To B. of Diocletian Church. Fall of Simon Magus. Meridian line,—Moslems in St. Sophia: transverse.[2]

Sunday March 15th. Attacked by singular pain across chest & in back. In my room till 5½ P. M. Dined at table d'hote. This day saw nothing, learned

[1]Melville used this identical phrase when he called on Page before. I cannot convince myself the reading is not correct, but I have no idea of Melville's intention.

[2]Though the reading of every word in this passage is certain except the last, I cannot resolve its mystery. I can only fall back upon quoting *Clarel* (Vol. 1, p. 324), where on the border of the Dead Sea Simon Magus is mentioned:

> And, yes, 'twas here—or else I err—
> The legend claims, that into sea
> The old magician flung his book
> When life and lore he both forsook:
> The evil spell yet lurks, may be.—

nothing, enjoyed nothing, but suffered something. *Monday March 16th* Vatican day.—Afterwards to Pincian. Could not engage seat in coupe of diligence. Have to go to Florence by Civita Vechia. haze Sistine Chapel—blue clouds, limbs.

Tuesday March 17th. To Frascati by R.R. Crossing Campagna by R.R.—Villa Alrdobrandini. Charming day & grounds. Avenues of trees. Laurel, cypress, pine, olive. Rich masses of foliage. Stone seats at angles. View of Tusculum (Cicero) from top of hill, at end of long avenue of olives. The cave-skull. The fountain, seen thiough hall of villa. Maps. Mellow aspect of all. Willows advanced as far as middle of May with us. Felt the bracing, reviving air of these hills very sensibly. Air of Rome hypochondriac.—Fine neglect of ground of villa. Omnibus ride, through Rome to & from R.R.

Wednesday March 18. Breakfasted on i6 pennies at Caffe Nuovo. To Torlonia Villa—small chambers —theaters—arbored dessert room—colonade & sea — rich decorations. — Grounds. The cave — the tournament—the artificial ruins—the circus &c&c. Grounds small. Fine view.—Crawfords[1] studio—

[1]Thomas Crawford (1814-1856) American sculptor. In 1835 he went to Rome, which he made his home, and became a pupil of Thorwaldsen. He married the sister of Julia Ward Howe, and was the father of Marion, the novelist.

Colossal America & various statues. Extent of studio. Indian, Backswoodsman &c &c

Thursday March 19th. Engaging vetturino for C. Vechia. Old stables &c.—To Villa Doria Pampili. Great Extent.—rich green—Paradise within Paradise. Yellow villa.—long vista of green & green water. The cedars & pines. Avenues of olives. View of St. Peters. The terrace gardens—the form of the par terre—flourishes of . . . .[1] Finer than English Park—richer foliage & sweeter atmosphere. Brilliant colorings & soft.—The Ghetto. The market (butcher) in old temple—alley leading through between columns. Filth & crowd. Old clothes—babies in basket & babies sewed up. Fountain of 7 branch candlestick. Way in which old temples are used—churches—shops—allies—blacksmiths, markets &c&c&c. View from piazza of San Pietro in Montano. Best in Rome. In the evening at Caffe Nuovo—old palace. Deep recesses of windows. Crowd of orderly well-dressed people. Magical guitar man. Hush & applause.

Friday March 20th. At 6. A. M started for Tivoli. Chill, grey ride across Campagna. Lake Tartarus.[2] Travertine.—Villa of Hadrian—Solemn scene & solemn guide—Extent of ruins,—fine site. Guide

[1]Undecipherable.

[2]Laga de' Tartari, near which are travertine quarries.

philosophizing.—Tivoli on heigth. Temple of the Nymph overhanging—paths—gallery in rock—Claude—not to Paradise, but Tivoli.—shading—middle tint—Villa of Mecanas.—Chill ride home in the evening.—

Saturday March 21st. Rainy. Run about getting my *vises.* Sam[1] left his card. Saw him. Had letter from home to 20th Feb. All well. Met to part.—At 4 P. M. started in veturino for Civitta Vecchia in company with Mr & Miss R. of New Jersey and an Italian lady. Desolate ride across desolate country. (Last view of St. Peters. Went out by gate near it.) At midnight stopped for three hours at lonely inn. Heard Meditterranean near. Rode on.

Sunday March 22d Arrived at C. Vecchia at 6 A. M. Crowds in streets. Sheepskin leggins &c. At 3 P. M. went aboard French steamer "Aventime", small craft. Great crowd. Turkish flag hoisted in honor of Turk envoy to Sardinia. Talked with him. His views of Mohammedanism &c. Upper classes of Turkey indulge philosophical opinions upon religion, &c. Repeated story of Abbots fire at Salonica. Same as I heard from Abbot himself.—Slept on settee (no berth).

Monday March 23d At Leghorn by daylight. Pleasant morning, though damp. Passports. Nothing

[1]Samuel Shaw, mentioned earlier on p.127.

special about Leghorn. At 10½ took 2d class cars for Pisa. Walked at once to the Duomo &c———— One end of it looks like coral grottos in sea,—pearl diver, pillars in tiers. —St Peter's uplifted arm handle of bronze door.—*Baptistery* like dome set on ground. Wonderful pulpit of marble.—Campanile[1] like pine poised just ere snapping. You wait to hear crash. Like Wadsworth's moon cloud, it will move altogether if it move at all, for Pillars all lean with it. About 150 of 'em. There are houses in wake of fall.—*Campo Santa.* Beauty of bowered walks of stone. Frescoes. Wags who painted them. Tartarus —tooth-pulling—serpent looking in eye. Impudent —mouth. Esop might have designed it. The three kings.—The four monuments stand in commons—grass. grown out of ground. Came upon them as upon bouquet of architecture.

[Interior of duomo magnificent. St. Agnes. &c.

[Sea-chapel on river side. Collonaded street.

Silence of the Common. & River-side. At 5½ P. M took cars for Florence. Level plain richly cultivated. Mountains. At 8 P. M arrived at Florence. Hote du Nord. Caffe Doney near it. To bed early, no sleep for 2 nights past.

Tuesday March 24th. Cold & raining all day. To Pitti Palace—"It's as bad as too much pain: it

[1]See *Pisa's Leaning Tower* (*Poems*, p. 279).

gets to be pain at last" Heard this broken latter part of sentence from wearied lady coming from Ufezzi Palace.—She was talking no doubt about excess of pleasure in these galleries.—Florence is a lovely city even on a cold rainy day. Ufezzi Palace. The Perseus of Cellini. Wandered about after leaving gallery Pitti. To the Duomo & Campanile. Came upon them unexpectedly. Amazed at their magnificence. Could not enter. Bought fine mosaics for one Napoleon.—Breakfasted today at Caffe Doney.

Wednesday March 25th. Festa, galleries closed. To Pitti gardens, rather Boboli. Noble views of Florence & country. Strolled about generally to churches, piazzas, &c. At Santa Croce saw tombs of Dante, M. Angelo, Alfieri, and Machiavelli. Preacher near M.'s tomb. M. said naught. Crucifix held out towards him. Campo Santa here.—At Annunziata saw fine frescoes of A. del Sarto. Gamblers struck by lightning.—Animated appearance of streets. Walked over to Romana Gate, outside to Bellesgardo. Striking view from the hill of city & Vale d'Arno. Roundabout walk to get to it. Abruptly came upon it, by a narrow lane between high walls of gardens. The tower on the Vecchio palace the grand feature.—Came on violent rain; & walked home in it.

Thursday March 26th. Sunned myself after breakfast in Grand Ducal square. To the Uffizi Gallery. Idle to enumerate. Grand view of tower of Vechio palace from head of gallery. View of covered way that crosses the Vechio bridge.—Not pleased with the Venus de Medici, but very much astonished at the wrestlers & charmed with Titian's Venus. The Portraits of painters interesting.—To the Accademia di B. Arti.—Giotto's paintings. Rich effect of gilding & raised parts. These are predecessors of the Peruginos & Raphaels. Saw a large painting, not referred to in my hand book, which contained many faces, attitudes, expressions & groupings I had noted at Rome in Raphael. Undoubtedly Raphael took from this, or some yet older painting. But still more, the *whole spirit* was the same.—Could not get access to all parts of the Accademia.—But saw the statues,—such as they are. Returning, passed Ricardi palace—Immense arched & lowering pile, with massive and impending cornice. Raining pretty much all day, at times violently.—At dinner table accosted by singular young man who speaks 6 or 8 languages. He presented me with a flower, and talked like one to whom the world was delightful. May it prove so.

Friday March 27th. At Caffe after breakfast sat musing upon caffes in general, & the young men frequenting them. Something good might be written on the "Caffe Doney", including that "Henry" & the flower-girls.—To the Museum of Natural History. Immense collection. Lapis lazuli—chrystal vessels, dragons, perfumes[1] &C&cc. Wax plants, seeds & germinations. Anatomical preparations. Terrible cases & wildernesses of rooms of them.—The Sicilian's work. No 1. Interior of case, broken arches, skeleton thrown under arch—head of statue—dead expression—crown & sceptre among bones—medallions—Death & scythe—pointing—tossed skeletons & tools. horrible humiliation. Cleft shows ruined[1] temples & pyramid.

No. 2. Vault—heaps—all colors from deep green to buff—all ruinous—detached bones—mothers children old men, intricacy of heaps. Man with cloth over face bringing down another body whose buff contrasts with the putrid green.

No. 3. In a cavernous ruin. Superb mausoleum like Pope's, lid removed shows skeleton & putridity. Roman sarcophagus—joyous triumphal procession—putrid corpse thrown over it.—grating—rats, vampires—insects. slime & ooze of corruption.—Moralist, this Sicilian. (—[2]) The final collection.—

[1]Tentative reading.

[2]Here, between parentheses, is a single letter (or figure) that looks like a cross between an M and a H.

Revisited Pitti Gallery. The 3 Fates of M. Angelo. Admirable expression. The way the one Fate looks at other—Shall I?—The expectancy of the 3d. (Transition from splendid humanity of Gallery to the Sicilian) The inlaid tables & pictures. S. Rosa's portraits (one autograph) Battle Peice.—To Powers'[1] studio. His America. Il Penseroso, Fisher Boy.—Saw him. Open, plain man. Fine specimen of an American.—To the Cascine.—Dined at the Luna with the young Polyglot. Walk along river & home.

Saturday 28th March. Before breakfast ascended Duomo. Entered Ball. Fine morning & noble view. Parapet round the building. Fresco of dome. Immense foot five feet long by measurement.—Magnitude of Dome.—After breakfast at Caffe Doney, did some business & then to Ufizzi gallery for last look. Afterwards to Fiesole. Boccaccio's Villa—Medici villa. Franciscan convent. View from windows. Old maps,—behind the age.—Etruscan wall. —To the Cascine & home. After dinner packed carpet bag & wrote this.

Sunday 29th April. Porter forgot to wake us at 3. A M. Diligence started without us. Ran round the Duomo to the Gate. All day among hills. Crossed

[1]Hiram Powers (1805-1873), an American sculptor who established himself in Florence in 1837. Melville mentions his most important works.

the Appenines. Grand scenery. Long reaches of streams through solitary vallies. No woods. No heartiness of scenery as in New. England. Drawn by oxen part of the way. 4000 feet above sea. Deep banks of snow in places. Lonely houses. Villages. Grave & decorous people: breakfast in the huts.[1] Nothing of talk in the coupè; But much smoking: *Monday March 30th.* Stopping at the "Three Moons". Fine day. Saw the leaning tower—black & grimy—brick. Its companion is of prodigious heigth. To the Gallery. The Madonna of the Rosary. A Circe. St. Cecilia. David Victorious. &c. —To the Campo Santa—Vast extent of sepulchral arcades. Splendor of some of the monuments. Arcade winding up the hill to church—three miles. Saw the University. The court all coats of arms of students. Statue of the learned lady. Walked under the arcades in the evening. First thing at Bologna, tried Bologna sausage, on the principle that at Rome you first go to St. Peters.

Tuesday March 31st. After breakfasting with the young C.[2] Traveller at caffe, started alone in diligence for Padua.—Polite elderly gentleman in diligence. A dead level country in strong contrast to last Sunday's travel. Ponds for hemp. Vineyards.

[1]Doubtful reading.
[2]Commercial?

Stone farm-houses & stone barns without sides.—At one P. M. came to Ferrara, where diligence stopped till 3. Went to see cathedral. Interesting old pile. Portico sustained by pillars resting on old hunchbacks. — The Last Judgement sculptured overhead. The Father in the angle of pediment. Below to right & left the elect & reputable. The four figures stepping out of their stone graves, as out of bed. The legs thrown out in various attitudes. Capital. Grotesque figures.—Fine bell-tower, but incomplete.—The old palace of the ancient counts of Ferrara is surrounded by broad moat. Drawbridge &c. Massy brick arches over moat.—Ferrara is on a dead plain, grass grows all about, seems a human common.—Tasso's prison. Mere cider-cellar. Grated window, but not strong. Byron's name &c. Other scribblers.—From Ferrara to Padua went by smaller post. Austrian. Old fashioned vehicle. Mysterious window & face. Secret recesses. Hide. Old fashioned feelings. Crossed the Po, quite a broad stream & very turbid & rapid. Yellow as Mississippi. Alluvial look. Old ferry boat. Austrian frontier. At dusk came to Rovigo, a considerable town. Saw two more leaning towers there; Dismantled & . . . . .[1] At midnight came to Padua, & to the hotel "Star of the East".

[1]Illegible.

Wednesday April 1st. Rainy day. To the famous caffe of Pedrocci. Worthy of its fame, being of great size and well furnished. Got a grave dark guide & started with great-coat & umbrella to see the sights —To the town hall. Wonderful roof (India) To the . . . . . .[1] palace to see the "Satan & his host."[2] Fine attitude of Satan. Intricate as heap of vermicelli. Church of St. Antony[3] & Shrine. Superb. Crutches & pictures. Bronze bas-reliefs. Goliath & David, &c. Promenade.—The Brenta flowing round it. Pleasant aspect of Brenta winding through town. To Giotto's chapel.—The Virtues & Vices. Capital. The Scriptural pictures.—The Arena.—Fine church in vicinity. Old Palaces & old arches & old streets. At 2. P. M took cars for Venice. Raining hard. Comfortable cars.—Level country. Approaching Venice like approaching Boston from the West.—Into gondola to Hotel Luna.[4] Dined at table'dhote, & sallied out to piazza of St. Marco, & about there till 8 P. M.

[1]Illegible. The same word occurs earlier on p.131.

[2]Melville is pretty certainly referring to Giotto's *Last Judgment.* On the entrance wall of the chapel of the Madonna dell' Arena.

[3]Which may have provoked the verses *In a Church of Padua* (*Poems*, p. 279).

[4]Opposite the royal garden, close to the South West side of the Piazza of St. Mark.

April 2d, Thursday. Breakfasted at Florian's, on roll. Went into St. Mark's. Ducal Palace. Oily looking interior, reeking look, disappointed. Repairing dome-scaffold. To Rialto. Up Bell Tower. In gondola to Grand canal & round by Guidecca.[1] Dinner. Walk to St. Mark's. To bed.—No place like the St. M.s Square for enjoyment. Public ball rooms — no hours. Lights. Ladies taking refreshments outside (In morning they breakfast on sunny side). Musicians. Singers. Soldiers &c &c &. Perfect decorum. Fine architecture.—In the evening met in Ducal Palace (the court) affable young man (Antonio) engaged him to meet me for guide tomorrow. *April 3d Friday*. To Glass bead manufactury. Drawing the rods like twine-making. Cutting, rounding, polishing, coloring a secret. To Gold chain manufactury. Old Venetian gold. Various gold . . . . .[2] To Church St. Giovanni Paolo.[3] Mounments. The chapel with the beautiful bas-relief. Christ expounding to the doctors. To the Arsenal. Great basins. Turks standard. Lanterns. On the canals. Othello's house & statue. Shylocks. L. Byron's. Foscari Palace. Fine view of G. Canal.—After dinner in Piazza.

[1]An adjacent island, to the South.
[2]Illegible.
[3]See the opening chapter of *Stones of Venice*.

April 4th, Saturday. Breakfast at Mindel's. Took gondola at Piazzetta for Murano.[1] Village in water. passed cemetery,[2] on isle.—Gliding in to water village. Old church. Back & to Jesuit Church. Marble drapery of pulpit. Astonishing what can be done with marble. Into Grand Canal. House of gold. Duke of Budin's.[3] Dutchess de Berris[4] &c&c. Hotel de Ville—old palace—superb court, & stair case. Frescoes of courtiers looking down & over balustrade beyond stair case.—To the bankers & Giudecca Canal. To Gallery, Titian's Assumption. The great black heads & brown arms. St. Mark coming to rescue. Venetian noble. Old pictures of Venice.—Grand saloons.—Titians Virgin in the Temple. After dinner, took gondola till dark on Canals. Old Palace with grinning monsters &c. Bought coat. To bed at 9½.

April 5th. Sunday. Breakfast on St. Marks. Austrian flags flying from their masts. Glorious aspect of the basilica in the sunshine. The charm of the square: The snug little breakfast there. Ladies. Flower girls —musicians. pedlers of Adriatic shells. Cigar stores &c &c.—Sat in a chair by the arcade at Mindel's

[1]An island about a mile and a half North of Venice.

[2]The Cemetery Island (Cimitero), half way to Murano.

[3]I have been unable to confirm this name, or identify the palace.

[4]Palazza Vendramin Calergi.

some time in the sun looking at the flags, the sun, & the church. (The shadow of the bell-tower.[1] The Pigeons. People coming to feed them.—Took gondola. To the Garden laid out by Napoleon. At end of Venice. (Like Battery at N. York) Fine view of lagoon & isles on two sides of Venice. To the Lido, from whence fine view of Venice, particularly the Ducal palace &c. Walked across the sand to the Adriatic shore. Calm waters. Long wide beach.—Through the grassy lagoon to Armenian Convent. Admirable retirement from the world, asleep in the calm Lagoon, the Lido a breakwater against the tumultuous ocean of life.—Garden, convent, quadrangles, cloisters,—View from library window—isles—The city in the distance. Portraits of noble bearded old Armenian priests. Old printing presses. Turkish medal. M.S.Bible. Chapel. 8 worshippers. & 8 priests. Superb vestments, blended with superb light streaming in from shining lagoon through windows draped with rosy silks. Chaunting, swinging silver censers—puff of incense at each worshipper. Great gorgeousness of effect.—The approach, gliding in—between grass.—Smell of stale incense peculiar to these old Churches. Only found out this—the cause of it—today.—Back to the city. Mirage-like effect of fine day—floating in

[1]In pencil, above the line: *Walking in it.*

air of ships in the Malamocco Passage, & the islands. To the church of Santa Maria Salute. Octagonal. To the church of S. Giorgio Maggiore. Series of carvings in wood. Landed at steps of Ducal palace under Bridge of Sighs. Prison blackened as by fire. Also palace in parts. Was a fire here. Walked in piazza of St. Mark. Crowds of people promenading. Pigeons. Walked to Rialto. Looked up & down G. Canal. Wandered further on. Numbers of beautiful women. The rich brown complexions of Titian's women drawn from Nature, after all. (Titian was a Venetian) The clear, rich, golden brown. The clear cut features, like a cameo. —The vision from the window at end of long, narrow passage.[1]—Walked by moonlight & gaslight in piazza of St. Mark. Number of singers, & musicians.—The tumblers & comic actors in the open space near Rialto. The expression of the women tumblers.—The Ducal palace's colonade like hedge of architecture.—On these still Summer days the fair Venetians float about in full bloom like pond lilies.—G. Canal not straight & stiff, but irregular with projections for advantageous fronts. Winds like a Susquehanna. View from balcony of Foscari palace. Best site. Huge suites. Occupied as barrack.

[1]Is the strange poem *In a Bye-Canal*, in *Timoleon* (*Poems*, pp. 277-8) in recollection of this?

Austrian cots & burnishing armor. Cooking & scrubbing in great hall.—On the canals of Venice all vehicles are represented. Omnibus, private coach, light gig, or sulky, pedler's cart, hearse.—[You, at first, think it a freshet, it will subside, not permanent,—only a temporary condition of things. —St: Mark's at sunset. Gilt mosaics, pinnacles, looks like holyday affair. As if the Grand Turk had pitched his pavilion here for a summer day. 800 years! Inside, the frescoes, marbles, from extreme age, look like a mural[1] of rare old soaps.—have an unctuous look. Fairly steamed with old devotions as refectories with old dinners.—In Venice nothing to see for the Venetians.—Rather be in Venice on rainy day, than in other capital on fine one.—My Guide. How I met him, & where. Lost his money in 1848 Revolution & by travelling.—Today in one city, tomorrow in next. Fine thing to travel. When rich, plenty compliment How do you do, Antonio—hope you very well, Antonio—Now Antonio no money, Antonio no compliment. Get out of de way Antonio. Go to the devil, Antonio. Antonio you go shake yourself. You know dat Sir, dat to de rich man, de poor man habe always de bad smell? You know dat Sir?

Yes, Antonio, I am not unaware of that. Chari-

[1]Melville wrote *mura*.

tably disposed. Old blind man, give something & God will bless you [Will give, but doubt the blessing]. [Antonio good character for com. man] Did not want to die. Heaven. You believe dat? I go dere, see how I like it first.—His rich anecdote. Byron swimming[1] over by nunnery[2] to watch[3] a lady in palace opposite. The Prussian countess, countess sends. Very wicked lad but very happy.—Floating about philosophizing with Antonio the Merry. Ah, it was Pausillippo.—Whether saw the brother of E. of Austria or not.—Leaning over parapet. Boys. silver lace. Anxious to settle it; & in my favor, for I consider that some of the free democracy would not look with disrespect upon the man who had &c &c &c.

April 6th. Left Venice at 5½ A M for Milan. Through Padua & Vicenza to Verona, where bride & groom entered the cars. Verona & Brescia had noble views of Lago di Garda, with Mount Baldus in distance. Villages upon its shore & on an island. Long vista of the lake between great overlapping mountains whose snows insensibly melted into the purples. Passed to the north continually by the first series of the Alps. R. R. over dead level of

[1]Or *sunning;* though either is tentative.
[2]Very tentative.
[3]Very tentative; *wake* seems as likely.

Lombardy plain. Rich cultivation. Mulberry trees, vines. Farm houses so unlike ours. No signs of hard work as with us. This region the scene of Napoleon's campaigns. At Coccaglio took diligence for Treviglio (18 m. from Milan). Rode from 1 P M till 6. In coupe. Arrived at Milan at 7½ P. M. Omnibus to Hotel de le Ville. Row at station between cabman & Austrian gen d'arms. Walked out to see the cathedral by night. Tour of shops &c A Canal.

April 7th Tuesday. To the Gallery. Very extensive, and some noble paintings. St. Catherine's Martyrdom. St. Mark at Alexandria is admirable for accuracy of architecture costume & expressiveness. To the Camp d'Armo. Arch. To the picture of Leonardo da Vinci. In suburb of Milan. Curious old brick church. Very old. Some trouble finding the refectory. At last directed to an archway where stood trumpeters. *Not* for Leonardo, though. Led through passages occupied by military (cavalry) to large court (like that of inn). Refectory a long, high, blank room, two ends painted. Great stage for copyists. Catching last hues of sunset. Whole picture faded & half gone. (Photograph copy of it I saw)—Significance of the Last Supper. The joys of the banquet soon depart. One shall betray me, one of you—men so false—the glow of sociability is so evanescent, selfishness so lasting.—Leonardo & his oil, case of a great man (Wordsworth) & his theory. To the cathedral. Glorious. More satisfactory to me than St. Peters. A wonderful grandure. Effect of burning window at end of aisle. Ascended,—Far below people in the turrets of open tracery look like flies caught in cobweb.—The groups of angels on points of pinnacles, & everywhere. Not the conception but execution. View from summit. Might . . . . . [1] host of heaven upon top of Milan Cathedral. Dined at 5 P. M. at table dhote of the Hotel de la Ville. Curious old gentleman there. Prided himself upon filling his glass. Young man. Talk. About cathedral.

April 8th Wednesday. Up at 5. A M. At 6½ started for Lake Como. Ride of hour & half in cars over dead rich plain. Took steamer at Como. Like going to Lake George.—Wonderful populousness of shores of Lake. Abrupt rise of mountains. roads cut through rocks, ravines,[2] ledges. View at Belleaggio of the three arms of the lake. Mountains

[1]Though Melville has a poem on *Milan Cathedral* (*Poems*, p. 280) in which he speaks of "the host of heaven" it gives no solution to this undecipherable word.—Any alert reader must feel both piqued and impatient, I am sure, at such lacunae as this. Even half-wits, it would seem, after not too prolonged an agony, couldn't avoid stumbling upon an obvious and certain reading. It may be I have erred in not consulting the half-wits.

[2]Tentative reading.

rolled together in watery blue. Snow upon summits. Picturesque boats boating at every village. Villages upon all kinds of sites. Some midway upon steep slopes as if they had slipped there in a landslide. Churches on isolated peaks. Groups of hamlets—pinfolds. Villages by scores, or hundreds. Terraced vegetation. Lone houses way up, here & there. Cascades, (under house) No trees. Back to Milan at 7 P. M.

Thursday April 9th. Up at 5. Scribbled here, and down to breakfast at 6½. at hotel. Young Parisian and lady there. At 9. o'clock started in diligence for Novara. Smart postilions, bugles under arm, glazed hat, metal band, jack boots. Over dead flat Lombardy plains, Alps in sight to the North. Passed many populous villages & towns. High cultivation of a most fertile soil. Crossed noble granite bridge of the Ticino. Came to Novara at 1½. Lunched there. Remained, waiting for train, 4 hours. Walked in boulevard on old walls—ancient brick fortress with deep, broad moat—Old duomo. Thorvaldsen's angels. Old court. Baptistry. Wax works. Nails & hammer, hair &c. At 5½ took train for Turin. Fell in with Greek from Zephalonia ("English subject") Arrived at Turin 9. P. M. Adventure with omnibus, porters, and Hotel d la Europe.—At Novara, saw church with wooden architecture before it. Within, altar made into stage where were pasteboard figures of scriptural characters. Exactly as in theatre. And lighted.

Friday April 10th. Very rainy. Breakfasted at caffee (gilded octagonal saloon) in Via di Po. Walked under the great arcades. Took view across to Colina. Visited Gallery. Admirable painting of "A Confessional". Some heads of Titian. 4 fine allegorical paintings—Earth, Air, Fire, Water. Ruben's Magdalen—excellently true to nature, but very ugly. Groups of children by Van Dyke—six in a row, heads—charming. Teniers tavern scenes. The remarkable Teniers effect is produced by first dwarfing, then deforming humanity. Breughel—always pleasing.—Piazzo Castello, where hotel is, is the centre of Turin. Interesting old pile, with various fronts, and grotesque assemblage of various architectures. Turin is more regular than Philadelphia. Houses all one cut, one color, one heigth. City seems all built by one contractor & paid for by one capitalist[1]—Singular effect of standing in arch of castle, & looking down vista of Via di Grossa to Mount Rosa & her snows.—Caught it unobscured by clouds early on the morning I left Turin.—Boulevards around the town. Many caffes & fine ones—Laboring people & poor women taking

[1]Which, indeed, in the founding of the city, was true.

their frugal breakfast in fine caffes. Their decorum, so different from corresponding class at home.—In the evening it cleared off. Went down to the Po again. Stood on steps of church there. To bed early.

Saturday April 11th. Bright weather. Up early to see Mount Rosa from the street. Saw it. Breakfasted on chocolate (Turin famous for it) on bank of Po. At 10 A. M. took cars for Genoa, over 100 miles. Pleasant for some time & passed through pleasant country. Very populous & highly cultivated. Approaching Appennines, noble scenery. Road built with great skill & cost. Numerous tunnels through hills at base of Appennines, till at last comes the Grand Tunnel—2 miles long.—Arrived at Genoa in rain at 3 P. M. Carpet bag fell from shoulder of clumsy porter. Afraid to look at Kate's[1] affairs.—Stopped at hotel Feder on water side. Walked through Strada Nuova &c. Palaces inferior to those of Rome, Florence, & Venice. One peculiarity is the *paintings of architecture* instead of the reality. All kinds of elaborate architecture represented in fresco.—Machiavelli's saying that the appearance of a virtue may be advantageous, when the reality would be otherwise.—Streets like those of Edinburgh; only still more steep & crooked. Ascended

[1]His sister, Catherine Gansevoort Melville (1825-1905). In 1853 she had been married to John C. Hoadley.

one for view.—Dined at table 'dhote. Fine room. The hotel occupies old palace. In evening walked on . . . . . [1] nigh port. Lofty hotels. Tower of the Cross of Malta. View of hills in distance.

Sunday April 12th. Breakfasted at Caffee. Chocolate. To the Public Promenade on ramparts. Look off. Troops. Unhandsome set of men. To the Cathedral. White & black marble in alternate courses. The steps. The *Gridiron* bas-relief. Fine interior. Tower. —The Ducal Palace. All the world out. Numbers of women. The Genoese head dress. Undines and Maids of the Mist. Simple & graceful. Receipt for making a plain women look lovely. Took omnibus (2 sous) to end of harbor. Lighthouse (300 feet high) Ascended. Superb view. Sea coast to south. Promontory. All Genoa & her forts before you. The heigth & distances of these forts, their outlying loneliness. The bleakness, the savageness of glens between, seem to make Genoa rather the capital and fortified camp of Satan: fortified against the Archangels. Clouds rolling round ramparts aerial. &c. Took the East side of harbor, and began circuit of the 3d line of defences. Ramparts overhanging the open sea, arches thrown over ravines. Fine views of sections of town. Up & up. Galley-slave prison. Gratings commanding view of

[1]Undecipherable.

sea—infinite liberty. Followed round & round. Nonplussed. Got to Public Promenade. Struck up steep lane to little church (fine view of sea from porch) Thence higher, and came to ramparts. Magnificent views of deep valley other side— & of Genoa & sea. Up & up. Finer & finer, till I got to the apex fort. Saw the two encircling vallies, and the ridge in which their heads unite to form the site of the highest forts. Great populousness of these vallies. Loneliness of some of the higher forts. Grounds enclosed by 3d circuit. Deep, woodless glens. Solitary powder magazines. Lonesome as glen in Scotch highlands.—With great fatigue descended irregular path, coming out by Doria palace. Dined at table d hote. Greek next me. Gigglers opposite.—Walked over the port. Stopped in with Greek at garden-caffee. Beautiful spot with fountains arcades &c &c &c. In bed at 8½.—Threatening rain all day, but none.

Monday April 14th Chocolate at Caffe. Old Wall of the Custom House. Visited the palaces. Different style from those of Rome &c. Large halls, preceding courts. But see Guide Book. Was shown thro' some palaces in great haste. Rosso palace in particular. Very windy. To hotel early, effects of yesterday's walk. Met Purser of Constitution at dinner. In bed by eight.

Tuesday Ap 15th Took cars at six A. M for Arona on Lake Maggiore. Met Lieutenant Fountleroy at station. Pleasant ride across new country. At 2 P. M sailed from Arona in (Passed thro' Allessandia & Novara) small steamer. Cold passage. Scenery fine. White-wash brush. Confusion of seasons. Pourings of cascades, Numbers of hamlets. The terraced isle. Came to Magadino at 7 P. M. Diligence to Bellizzona. Entered defile at dusk, and kept in it. Shadowy & vague approach among the roots of Alps. At Bellizona out jumped Dr Lockwood just from Simplon. *April 16.* At 2 A M started in diligence for crossing the San Gothard. Bow window. Silence, mystery. Steady roll of wheel. Dawn, zig-zags, Gorge, precipice, snow. At Airolo breakfasted. Mr Abbot accosted me. Storming violently. Hand sleds. Parties waiting at Airolo for three days. Started. Long train. Zig-zag. Houses of refuge. Discussion of the gods &c. Verge & brink of paths. Summit. Hospice. Old stone warehouse. Scene there. Men in comforters, frozen bones. Sledging goods.—Started again. Stoppage by goods coming the other way. Turning out. Floundering of horses. Descent. Like coming from the clouds. Noses of crags thrusting out—10000 feet. Down at Andermatt. Wet through. Diligence. Devil's Bridge. Scenery through Gorge. Green & white of grass &

snow. Lime torrent. Altdorf. Fluellen at 7 P. M.—*April 17*—Before breakfast next morning went out for view of Lake Lucerne—Bay of Uri. Chapel. (seats Methodists) at 9. A. M. started for Lucerne in steamer. Entrance of Bay of Uri. Tell's Chapel. At 11 came to Lucerne.—Thorswalden's lion—living Rock. Ramble with Abbot & fine views. Old Bridges. *Friday April 18.* At 8 A M started in diligence for Berne. Coupe, only Abbot & me. Charming day & charming country. Swiss cottages. Thrift neatness &c. Dinner at inn. At 7 arrived at Berne, putting up at "The Crown". Went to terrace of cathedral for view of Bernese Alps. There they were—seen over the green.

Saturday April 19th. Walk on terrace. Cathedral. Spent whole day almost with Mr. Fay—Abbot & daughter. Ride. Noble views of Alps. Rail Road building.

Sunday April 20th. At 10. A M. started in diligence (interior) for Basle. Fine day. At Soleure[1] dined. Encountered a Mr Smyth merchant of N.Y. Superb views of the Bernese Alps & Jura ranges all morning. Beyond Soleure drew near Jura,—palisades—About high as Saddle Back.[2] 4000 feet. Old castles.

[1]Or Solothurn.

[2]In the Berkshires. Melville's place at Pittsfield had been Saddle Meadows before he rechristened it Arrowhead. Saddle Meadows, incidentally, is the home of Pierre.

Entered by a remarkable defile. View of whole Alps through defile. Ride across.—Took R.R at L(augenbrüch)[1] and at 8 P. M put up at "The Wild Man" in Basle. Walked out, crossed the Rhine by bridge of boats. Deep, broad, rapid.

Monday April 21. At 5 A. M. off by R.R. for Strasbourgh—90 miles. To the Cathedral. Pointed—pinnacles—All sprouting together like bed of (asparagus)[2] what you call it? Brown free stone—the clock &c. Crowd waiting. Ascent. Not fine as Milan. Platform on top. The Spire. inscriptions (1500) At 2 P. M. crossed with Mr Smyth to Kiel. Passports. French & German. Baden. Took cars for Heidelburgh. Californians. Lovely afternoon. Level country bounded by hills. Great fertility. Getting the crops in. At 8 P M arrived at Heidelburgh. Hotel Adler.

Tuesday April 22. Up at 5 and mounted to Castle. Blossoms, grass, all things fresh round the charming old ruin. The chimney. Vault. View of Necker. The University.—The clover risen. trees sprouting. defile in ruins.—Flower bed in banquet hall. Knights in green niches.—Students. Daguerrotypes. At 2 P. M. took cars for Frankfort on Maine. At station encountered Dr Abbot again—bound to

[1]Melville gives the first letter and a dash.

[2]Above the line.

Frankfort. Same level fertile country as all way from Basle. At 4 P M came to Frankfort, stopping at hotel . . . .[1] After dinner Smyth invited us to ride about town.—Goethe's statue. Faust's. Cathedral. Luther's preaching place. River side. Park. Jews quarter. Rothschilds house. &c&c&c.

Wednesday Apl 23.—After breakfast went in to see Abbot—found him smoking in bed & better. Went to Rothschilds.—Eminent hard-ware merchant. Aspect of cash-room. kegs, barrels, rolls, presses, weights & scales, coopers, carmen & porters. Drove about the town. Faust's statue. The "Ariadne" of H . . . . . Rose light. Beauty and Deformity contrasted. At half past eleven A. M. started in cars for Wiesbaden, but by mistake arrived in Mayence—at 2 P. M. Took boat for Cologne. Mayence on low land, but covering large space, fine cathedral & buildings. Passed through Hoch-land. Plenty of vineyards (sticks) down Rhine. Got to Cologne at 10 P. M. Rainy & cold all day. My partial companion. (from Boston?) Stopped at Hotel de Cologne.

Thursday April 24th At 5 o'clock got up, breakfasted & went to R.R. station, across river for Amsterdam. Through Dusseldorf & Utrecht. Rainy, cold, hail at times & sleet. Rich country, level.—Entering Holland, began to look like a great heath—passed

[1]Melville left a blank.

much waste, brown, muddy looking land—immense pastures, light green. Adventure after hotel in Amsterdam, where we arrived at 3½ P. M. Put up at last at the "Old Bible", upon which something good might be written in the ironical way. *April 24th* (Mistake of a day before). Very cold & snowy yesterday afternoon. At ordinary a number of sea captains. This morning got a queer little old Dutchman for guide & went to Picture Gallery. Wonderful picture of Paul Potter—The Bear. (Rich handling of a Dutch Surgeon)[1]—The Syndics of Rembrandt & The Night Watch (shadows)—Portrait of a painter & his wife—admirable (Old Pedlers) The abandonment of good humored content. —Dutch convivial scenes. Teniers & Breughel.—Streets of Amsterdam like long lines of old-fashioned frontispieces in old folios & old quartoes. Canals & drawbridges. Greasy looking old fellows—Teniers. To the "Garden" & "Plantation". The pink-mouthed dog. The "Sloth".—View of city from cupola of palace. Red tiles of houses. The Port. The drop of gin.—Shape of Amsterdam like ampitheatre, water all round it.—Broeck,[2] did not see. place of

[1]I am very doubtful about the reading of every word in this phrase.

[2]Burdened with the reputation of being the cleanest town in the world.

cheese, butter, & tidiness.—The old galliot.[1] Neat, & chest of drawers.—At 4½ took train for Rotterdam. Smoking cars. One all to myself. Passed through Harlem—Neat, like "Colonee" in Albany. Leyden, big cathedral. The Hague. Arrived at Rotterdam at 7½. Got guide & went to Dance Houses. Into three of them. Striking & pathetic sight. The promenading girls—music—their expression & decorousness.—Villiany of the guide. To bed by 9½.

April 25th. With guide went to cathedral of St. Lawrence. (Forgot to say that while in Amsterdam visited the church there. Carved pulpit, &c but nothing inside) Fine view of Rotterdam & environs. House of Erasmus. At 11 oclock went on board steamer for London. Fair wind, but chilly. Passed several of the embankments.—The fat steward. At 7 oclock, strong, fair wind.

April 26th Monday. Made the mouth of Thames early, & steamed up, passed many objects of interest. The mammoth ship "Great Eastern". At 7 A M were at St. Catherine Wharf. Cab, & to Tavistock Hotel. Dreary Sunday in London. Walked to Hyde Park & in Kensington Gardens. Got an idea of them.

April 27th. To the Longman's &c

April 28th. To Madame Tussaud's. No where else in particular.

[1]See *Redburn*, Chapter XXXV.

April 29th 30th—May 1st—
Thursday, Friday & Saturday.—Lay a sort of water-logged in London.—Reverie at the "Cock".[1] Chrystal Palace—digest of universe. Alhambra—House of Pansi[2]—Temple of—— &c&c&c.—Comparison with the pyramid.—Overdone. If smaller would look larger. The Great Eastern. Pyramid.—Vast toy. No substance. Such an appropriation of space as is made by rail fence. Durable materials, but perishable structure. Cant exist 100 years hence.—Beautiful view from terraces of Chystal Palace.—Thames Tunnel.
Rode out in omnibus to Richmond. Several evenings at Hyde Park to see the equestrians. Fine & bold riding of the ladies. Poor devil looking over the rail.—Visited the Vernon & Turner galleries. Sunset scenes of Turner. "Burial of Wilkie". The shipwreck. "The Fighting ———[3] taken to her last berth."

[1]Where, in the winter of 1849, he had spent gayer hours. The letter of cousin Henry Sanford Gansevoort summarizing Melville's lecture on *Statuary in Rome* (this letter is quoted from in the Introduction, p.xiii.) shows that Melville concluded his speech with a rehearsal of this "Reverie at the 'Cock.' "

[2]In Pompeii.

[3]In *Battle-Pieces* (*Poems*, pp. 41-2), Melville has a poem on the word that he here leaves a dash for, and supplements it with a note that begins: "The *Temeraire*, that storied ship of the old English fleet, and the subject of the well-known painting by Turner," &c.

Sunday May 2d. Left London by R R for Oxford. Clear day. Rich country. Passed through Berkshire. Level & fertile. Windsor castle in distance. Saw Reading, shire town of Berkshire. At 11½ arrived at Oxford.—Most interesting spot I have seen in England. Made tour of all colleges. It was here I first confessed with gratitude my mother land, & hailed her with pride. Oxford to Americans as well worth visiting as Paris, tho' in a very different way. —Pulpit in corner of quadrangle. Deer. Garden girdled by river.—Meadows beyond. Oxen & sheep. Pastoral & collegiate life blended.—Christ Church Meadow. Avenue of trees.—Old reef washed by waves & showing detached parts—so Oxford. Ivy branch over portal of St. John intertwining with sculpture. Amity of art & nature. Accord. Grotesque figures. Catching rheumatism in Oxford cloisters different from catching it in Rome. Contagion in Pomfili Doria but wholesome beauty in Oxford. Learning lodged like a faun. Garden to every college. Lands for centuries never molested by labor. Sacred to beauty & tranquility. Fell's avenue. Has beheld unstirred all the violence of revolutions. &c.—Ship roof. Spanish chestnut. Dining halls. [Dormer window derived from gable, as spire from elevating & sharpening roof in snowy climates—final result of gradual process.—Stair case of Christ Church. Single pillar as on Paris chapel. Each college has dining room & chapel—on a par—large windows. Soul & body equally cared for.—Grass smooth as green baize of billiard table.—The picturesque never goes beyond this.—I know nothing more fitted by mild & beautiful rebuke to chastise the (presumptuous)[1] ranting of Yankees.—In such a retreat old Burton sedately smiled at men.—Improvement upon the monkish. As knights templars were mixture of monk & soldier, so these of monk & gentleman. [These colleges founded as men plant trees.—Belfry cant ring bells, &c. Music coming out of church as leads ooze out of . . . . . . picture.[2]—Stopped at the "Mitre" at Oxford.—High Street.

Monday May 3d. Left Oxford at 9 A. M for Stratford on Avon. Changed for horse railroad. Stopped at the "Red Horse".—Shakespeare's house—little old groggery abandoned.—cheerless, melancholy. Scrawl of names.—The church Tomb stones before altar, wife, daughter son-in-law.—New Place.—Walk to Hathaway cottage at Shottery. Level country.—

At 3½ went on stage to Warwick. Cold & windy. Wonderfully beautiful country.—(Edge Hill).—

[1]In pencil, above the line.

[2]This whole sentence baffles me.

Aspect of Castle nigh Avon. Walked about Warwick. Entrance very fine. Old gate &c. At 6½ took R.R. for Birmingham. Arrived before dark. Mob of chimneys. Like Newcastle-upon-Tyne. Stopped at Queen's. by R.R. Drove around town. City Hall fine building. Parthenon. To bed early.

Tuesday May 4th. At 6 A. M. took R R for Liverpool. Like riding through burnt district—standing columns of pines, smoking or with stars[1] of flame from top.—The Chimnies. Arrived at Liverpool at 12. M.—Secured my berth on "City of Manhattan" by paying balance. (*The "Grecian"*)[2] Got letters from Brown, Shipley & Co. Saw Hawthorne. Called on Mr Bright. Got presents. Trunk. Packed.

Wednesday May 5th. Fine day. At 10 A. M. got on board tender for steamer.—At 11½—off for home.

[1]Questionable reading.
[2]Along the right margin.

Frescoes of Travel *by* *Three Brothers* *Poet, Painter, and Idler*[1]	Rousseau Cicero Byron Haydon	Venice Olympus Parthenon Leonardo.

J. C. should have appeared in Tahiti[2]
—Land of palms.—
Palm Sunday—*Beautiful Gate.*

Jerusalem seen from Bethlehem Road.

Spinoza, Rothschild &c. &.

{ Goods laid up in mosque—Maccabees.
Same in Temple—(M. 2B. 3C.)[3] (Note)

Eclipse.

Noah after the Flood.

Cap. Pollard.
of *Nant.*

[1]*Idler* substituted for *Scholar.*

[2]This is elaborated in *Clarel* (Vol. 2, p. 232). Here Melville but expresses a sentiment in sympathy with Frederick II of Sicily, whose comment upon the Holy Land was: "Christ should have seen my Palermo!"

[3]II Maccabees, Chapter 3.

Subjects for

Roman Frescoes

{ A group of cypresses in Villa D'Este.
Whispering apart like Angelo's "Fates"

{ From *Tartarus to Tivoli*
is but a step or two.

{ The Cenci portrait[1]

{ Sixtus Vth — His obelisks &c Sprung from the people — What it was to be Pope in those days. No democracies—Only way of rising to preeminence —& wicked preeminence.—What he did in order to be this.

[1]Down to here, written in pencil.

178

OXFORD

(Transferred from small pocket book)

It was in Oxford that I confessed from the first, & with glad gratitude, my mother land.—Oxford to an American of taste as well worth seeing as Paris. —Pulpit in corner of quadrangle.—Deer—green gardens—water courses—sheep—meadows beyond. —Rafters of roof of cloister of Spanish cedar.— Spire offspring of peaked roof. Final result of elevating & sharpening a roof in snowy countries.

Dormer window of gable.

Meadows of Christ Church.

Old reef washed by waves—standing parts—so Oxford.—Ivy branch intertwining with twigs of sculpture over Gothic door.—Union of Art & Nature.

Contagion in Pamfili Doria, but *wholesome* beauty in Oxford. Learning in Oxford lodged like a baron Garden to every college. Lands for centuries never molested by sordid labor—profane hand of enterprise—sacred to beauty & tranquillity.

Fell's avenue of elms.

Every college has dining halls & chapel—soul & body equally provided for.

The picturesque in sculpture goes not beyond Oxford.

Grass smooth as green baize of billiard table.

179

I know nothing more fitted by a mild & beautiful rebuke to chastize the sophomorean pride of America as a new & prosperous country.

In such a retreat old Burton composed his book, sedately smiling at men.

They have beheld all revolutions unchanged.

Improvement upon the monastic cloister As knights-templers were half soldier . . . . [1] monk—so these half monk half gentleman.

These colleges founded as men plant trees—for posterity.

[1] Illegible.

[1]The Vatican (a volume)
Busts of Titus & Tiberius (side by side)
Rome.
Bitterness—Dead Sea. (*Bitterness of Death*)
[The cypresses in the Villa D'Este whispering like
Michael Angelo's "Fates"
"Dolce Niente" (Sung softly)

[1]This whole page is in pencil.

[Seeing is believing.

The pains lie among the pleasures like sand in rice, not only bad in themselves, but spoiling the good.

[1]*St Sophia*—Suspended from above like fully blossomed tulip from its stem.—

Coliseum. Great green hollow—restore it repeople it with all statues in Vatican. Dying & Fighting Gladiators.

Restoring ruins—

7 branch candlestick—Sculptor's criticism.

More imagination wanted at Rome than at home to appreciate the place. Uncomfortable splendors —palaces like dripping ice.—. . . . .[2]—St Paul's— malaria—Smyrna robe splendor in richest folds[3] *Ruins look as much out of place in Rome as in British Museum*. Rivers of . . . . water.

Vatican like long walks in great Park—arbored with arabesques.

Climate of Rome—winter—there is warmth at times but distinct cheerlessness—seem to receive it by reflex not directly: Rapid driving—priest run over—humanity[4]—public carriage. Tombs on "Appian"—sown in corruption, raised in grapes.

[1]From here on, this section is a series of scrawls in pencil, faint and blurred.

[2]Illegible.

[3]In *Clarel*, Melville speaks of "Pride's Smyrna robe" as if it were gorgeous but infected.

[4]Questionable reading.

De Leon Consul at Alexandria.

George Wood (Concord N.H.) Consul at Beyroot

Daniel Mc Cartan. Poughkeepsie.

G. C. Rankin Author of "*What is Truth?*"
E. I. U. S. Club
14 St James Square.